CRIME VICTIMS' GUIDE TO JUSTICE

CRIME VICTIMS' GUIDE TO JUSTICE

Mary L. Boland
Attorney at Law

Sourcebooks Inc.

Naperville, IL • Clearwater, FL

Published by: **Sourcebooks, Inc.**

Naperville Office
P.O. Box 372
Naperville, Illinois 60566
(630) 961-3900
FAX: 630-961-2168

Clearwater Office
P.O. Box 25
Clearwater, Florida 33757
(813) 587-0999
FAX: 813-586-5088

Cover Design: Andrew Sardina/Dominique Raccah
Interior Design and Production: Andrew Sardina, Sourcebooks, Inc.

This publication is designed to provide accurate and authoritative information in regard to the subject matter covered. It is sold with the understanding that the publisher is not engaged in rendering legal, accounting, or other professional service. If legal advice or other expert assistance is required, the services of a competent professional person should be sought.
From a Declaration of Principles Jointly Adopted by a Committee of the
American Bar Association and a Committee of Publishers and Associations

Library of Congress Cataloging-in-Publication Data
Boland, Mary L.
     Crime victims' guide to justice / Mary L. Boland
          p.   cm.
     Includes index.
     ISBN 1-57071-166-6 (pbk.)
     1. Victims of crimes — Legal status, laws, etc. — United States — Popular works.   2. Criminal procedure — United States — Popular works. I. Title.
KG9763.Z9B65   1997
344.73'03288 — dc21   97-12716
                                                                                                                         CIP

Printed and bound in the United States of America.

Paperback — 10 9 8 7 6 5 4 3 2 1

CONTENTS

ACKNOWLEDGEMENTS ix

USING SELF-HELP LAW BOOKS. 1

INTRODUCTION. 3

CHAPTER 1 THE CRIMINAL JUSTICE SYSTEM 5
    The Criminal Law
    The Criminal Justice System
    Types of Crimes
    Elements of Crimes
    The Offender
    The State's Case
    The Defense Case

CHAPTER 2 SURVIVING THE CRIMINAL JUSTICE SYSTEM 13
    The Impact of Crime
    Getting Help
    Victim-Assistance Programs
    Hotline Services
    Crisis Counseling
    The Crime Victim Advocate
    How to Find a Program
    What if There are No Local Programs?

CHAPTER 3 THE VICTIM IN THE CRIMINAL JUSTICE SYSTEM 19
    Family Members and Loved Ones
    Witnesses
    The Growth of Victims' Rights
    Constitutional Rights of Victims

Victim "Bill of Rights" Laws
The Right to Restitution
The Right to Compensation
The Right to Civil Justice
Case Management

CHAPTER 4 YOUR PRIVACY RIGHTS **31**
Protecting the Victim's Privacy
Your Rights and the Media

CHAPTER 5 REPORTING THE CRIME **35**
Contacting the Police
The Role of Hospitals and Medical Personnel

CHAPTER 6 THE POLICE INVESTIGATION **39**
The Victim Interview
The Crime Scene
The Detective's Role
The Rights of the Victim

CHAPTER 7 ARRESTING THE OFFENDER **45**
Identifying the Offender
Lineup Procedures
Unknown Offenders
Making the Arrest
What if Police Don't Make an Arrest?

CHAPTER 8 FILING THE CHARGE **49**
Who Makes the Decision to File?
Screening the Case
Methods of Charging
The Grand Jury
Time Limits
The Charges in Your Case

CHAPTER 9 PRETRIAL PROCEDURES **53**
The Role of the Judge
The Victim's Rights
The Right to a Speedy Trial
Arraignment — Defendant's Initial Appearance
Bail
Preliminary Hearing
Pre-Trial Motions

CHAPTER 10 PLEA BARGAINING **63**
Types of Plea Bargains
Procedures
The Victim's Role

CHAPTER 11 THE CRIMINAL TRIAL **67**
Defendant's Right to a Jury
Opening Statement
Evidence and Testimony
The State's Case
The Victim as a Witness
The Defense Case
Closing Statement

CHAPTER 12 THE VERDICT **75**
The Role of the Jury
The Bench Trial
A Verdict on Some of the Charges

CHAPTER 13 THE SENTENCE **79**
Sentencing Dispositions
The Sentencing Hearing
The Victim Impact Statement
What the Sentence Really Means
Violations of Sentencing Orders

CHAPTER 14 APPEAL **89**
Who Can Appeal?
What Happens to the Offender During an Appeal?
What Can an Appeals Court Do?
The Victim's Rights

CHAPTER 15 AFTER THE CRIMINAL TRIAL **91**
When It's Over
Release or Escape of the Offender

CHAPTER 16 RECOVERING DAMAGES **95**
Criminal vs. Civil Courts
Other Options for Recovery of Damages

CHAPTER 17 THE WHAT AND WHO OF A CIVIL LAWSUIT **99**
What is a Civil Suit?
Who are the Parties to the Suit?

What if the Defendant Sues the Victim?

The Burden of Proof

The Elements of Civil Suit

Theories

Causation

Common Defenses

Damages

The Effect of the Criminal Case on the Civil Suit

The Effect of a Civil Suit on the Victim

CHAPTER 18 THE HOW AND WHEN OF A CIVIL LAWSUIT **111**

Evaluating and Preparing the Case

The Time and Place to File

CHAPTER 19 OVERVIEW OF THE CIVIL COURT PROCESS **117**

Starting the Process

The Discovery Stage

Settling the Case

Presenting the Case

The Verdict, Judgment, and Post Trial Decisions

Enforcing the Judgment

CHAPTER 20 SELECTED ISSUES AND CASES **137**

Sexual Assault Victims

Domestic Violence Victims

Cases Against Third Parties

CHAPTER 21 THE ROLE OF LAWYERS **151**

Lawyers and Confidentiality

Finding a Lawyer

Fee Agreements

Working with the Lawyer

APPENDIX A SAMPLE FORMS **157**

APPENDIX B STATE-BY-STATE LAWS **167**

APPENDIX C LEGAL RESEARCH **199**

APPENDIX D RESOURCES **201**

ENDNOTES **205**

INDEX **207**

ACKNOWLEDGMENTS

Many people contributed over several years to the information which eventually made its way into this book. I most want to thank Katherine A. Newell, an excellent paralegal and researcher, for her time and invaluable assistance in gathering, typing, and editing the compilation of statutory materials cited in this book.

USING SELF-HELP LAW BOOKS

Whenever you shop for a product or service, you are faced with various levels of quality and price. In deciding what product or service to buy, you make a cost/value analysis on the basis of your willingness to pay and the quality you desire.

When buying a car, you decide whether you want transportation, comfort, status, or sex appeal. Accordingly, you decide among such choices as a Neon, a Lincoln, a Rolls Royce, or a Porsche. Before making a decision, you usually weigh the merits of each option against the cost.

When you get a headache, you can take a pain reliever (such as aspirin) or visit a medical specialist for a neurological examination. Given this choice, most people, of course, take a pain reliever, since it costs only pennies, whereas a medical examination costs hundreds of dollars and takes a lot of time. This is usually a logical choice because rarely is anything more than a pain reliever needed for a headache. But in some cases, a headache may indicate a brain tumor, and failing to see a specialist right away can result in complications. Should everyone with a headache go to a specialist? Of course not, but people treating their own illnesses must realize that they are betting on the basis of their cost/value analysis of the situation, they are taking the most logical option.

The same cost/value analysis must be made in deciding to do one's own legal work. Many legal situations are very straight forward, requiring a simple form and no complicated analysis. Anyone with a little intelligence and a book of instructions can handle the matter without outside help.

But there is always the chance that complications are involved that only an attorney would notice. To simplify the law into a book like this, several legal cases often must be condensed into a single sentence or paragraph. Otherwise, the book would be several hundred pages long and too complicated for most people. However, this simplification necessarily leaves out many details and nuances that would apply to special or unusual situations. Also, there are many ways to interpret most legal questions. Your case may come before a judge who disagrees with this analysis.

Therefore, in deciding to use a self-help law book and to do your own legal work, you must realize that you are making a cost/value analysis and deciding that the chance your case will not turn out to your satisfaction is outweighed by the money you will save in doing it yourself. Most people handling their own simple legal matters never have a problem, but occasionally people find that it ended up costing them more to have an attorney straighten out the situation than it would have if they had hired an attorney in the beginning. Keep this in mind while handling your case, and be sure to consult an attorney if you feel you might need further guidance.

INTRODUCTION

Nearly everyone will be affected by crime in some way during their lifetime. Television brings trials into our homes, and "court-watching" has become commonplace. Yet, beyond the media hype, a victim's rights are a mystery to most, and no one can exercise rights they don't know exist. Victims, their families, and supporters must learn about these laws and learn how and when to apply this knowledge.

This book will help you understand the criminal and civil court systems from the victim's perspective. It is intended to teach you how the criminal justice system functions, what your rights are as a victim, how to find help, and how to make the people who make the decisions about your case accountable to you. This book is also intended to help victims who are considering filing a civil lawsuit. It is a starting place, a basic guide to the maze of our civil court process.

Do not hesitate to demand justice as you travel from victim to survivor. And when your journey is complete, gather strength from your experience and think about how you can have an impact on your community to improve the treatment of future victims.

Chapters 1 through 15 discuss the criminal court process. Chapters 16 through 21 explain the civil court process, and other ways to go about obtaining compensation for your losses due to being a crime victim.

Appendix A contains examples of letters and forms. These either illustrate the type of forms you may encounter as a crime victim, or the type of forms you may find helpful to secure your rights.

Appendix B gives information about the laws of each state relating to crime victims.

Appendix C provides some basic information about legal research, in the event you want to go beyond what is covered in this book.

Appendix D lists addresses and telephone numbers that may be useful to you.

THE CRIMINAL JUSTICE SYSTEM 1

In colonial times, when a person committed a crime, it was considered to be an injury to the victim and the victim was entitled to prosecute the case. This system favored wealthy victims, however, because poorer victims did not have the financial resources to seek justice. To make the process fairer, the government took over the responsibility of prosecuting a person accused of committing a crime. Crimes began to be considered public wrongs committed against the community, rather than private wrongs committed only against the individual victim.

THE CRIMINAL LAW

There are federal laws and procedures which apply to cases prosecuted in the federal court system, but most crimes are prosecuted in the state court systems. Within constitutional limits, each state is free to enact its own criminal laws and procedural rules, and has the right to develop its own descriptions, definitions, and classification of crimes. For example, what is called "rape" in one state may be called "sexual battery" or "sexual assault" by another. A case where a perpetrator holds three people up at gunpoint and empties the cash register may be considered a single robbery in one state or three robberies in another. The theft of $50 may be a misdemeanor in one state, and a felony in another.

THE CRIMINAL JUSTICE SYSTEM

The criminal justice system is designed to deter the commission of crimes, investigate and prosecute crimes, and punish and attempt to rehabilitate convicted offenders. The "system" refers to a group of agencies which have responsibility for taking action at certain times in the case. The police take the report and investigate the crime, the prosecutor charges the accused and tries the case, the judge oversees the court process, and corrections personnel are responsible for the incarceration of the defendant. Each of these agencies are separate, and they have different goals and purposes. Sometimes they work together better than others. In recent years, police and prosecutors have joined together to form task forces or specialized units to improve the handling of certain types of cases.

TYPES OF CRIMES

The most common classifications of crime in the United States are misdemeanor and felony. Each state can determine which crimes are felonies and which are misdemeanors. One common method of categorizing crimes is by the length of sentence. The least serious crimes are called petty offenses or infractions in most states. Examples of typical petty offenses are:

- Traffic violations
- Disturbing the Peace
- Loitering

In most states the maximum sentence for a misdemeanor is one year, although a few permit two years. Examples of typical misdemeanors are:

- Assault
- Simple theft
- Trespassing
- Battery
- Public Indecency (exposure)
- Telephone harassment

A felony is a more serious crime, and can be punishable by longer prison terms, a life sentence, or even death. Examples of typical felonies are:

- Murder
- Rape and Sexual Assault
- Arson
- Forgery
- Drugs (certain kinds)

- Manslaughter
- Home Invasion
- Carjacking
- Theft (over a certain amount)
- Aggravated Stalking

ELEMENTS OF CRIMES

In order to constitute a crime, certain "elements" must be present. These will be stated in the laws. For example, a traditional first-degree murder requires proof of four elements:

1. Killing a person,

2. unlawfully (without a legally justifiable excuse),

3. intentionally, and

4. with malice aforethought (i.e., with prior planning).

If one or more of the elements is not present, it is not sufficient to charge the offense, although it may be possible to charge another lesser offense. For example, if the killing was unlawful (unauthorized) and intentional (not an accident), but malice aforethought (prior planning) was not present, it might still be charged as a lesser offense of second degree murder.

Every crime has its own definition. An example of a criminal statute defining the offense of residential burglary follows:

A person commits residential burglary who knowingly and without authority enters the dwelling place of another with the intent to commit therein a felony or theft.

The definition of "dwelling" is found at another section of this state's criminal code:

For the purposes of §19-3 of this Code, "dwelling" means a house, apartment, mobile home, trailer, or other living quarters in which at the time of the alleged offense, the owners or occupants actually reside or in their absence intend within a reasonable period of time to reside.

Thus, sometimes, in order to fully understand the required elements of an offense, research may disclose more than one statute or section of law.

THE OFFENDER

Once a person is accused of a crime, he or she becomes a "party" to the case and is entitled to the protection of the United States Constitution, and all laws which apply to persons charged with a crime. Everyone who participates in committing the crime can be charged with the offense. For example, if three carjackers steal your car, each can be charged even if only one has the gun or drives away. The others can be held "accountable" for the actions of the gun-wielding driver. An example of an accountability statute is:

A person is legally accountable for the conduct of another when:

Either before or during the commission of an offense, and with the intent to promote or facilitate such commission, he solicits, aids, abets, agrees or attempts to aid, such other person in the planning or commission of the offense.

JUVENILES Teenage and younger offenders are responsible for a large percentage of the crimes committed in the United States today. Until recently, however, juveniles who committed crimes were considered "delinquent" and sent to a special juvenile court for processing. Most state laws still only permit criminal convictions against older teen offenders on the theory that younger children are not fully responsible for their conduct.

Some states do permit transfer to an adult court of a juvenile who commits a particularly violent or brutal crime.

FAMILY
MEMBERS

Family members can, and do, commit crimes against one another. Most often, the crimes of violence are called "domestic violence," but family members commit a range of criminal acts against one another. Technically, the criminal law does not distinguish between a family member offender and a stranger, but in fact, the criminal justice system seems to treat crimes committed by family members as being less serious. For many years, the criminal justice system treated crimes between family members as private disputes, and not public wrongs. Concepts of "private family matters" sometimes do affect charging decisions and sentencing options for family member offenders.

THE STATE'S CASE

In our system of justice, a criminal defendant is always presumed innocent. Therefore, in all cases, the state has the entire burden of proving "beyond a reasonable doubt" that a crime was committed and that the defendant committed the crime. The defense has no burden of proof in a criminal case. The Fifth Amendment to the Constitution guarantees that the defendant cannot be made to incriminate him or herself. That is why the defendant does not have to testify.

In the majority of cases, the testimony of a single witness is legally sufficient to convict a defendant in a criminal case.

Even circumstantial evidence may be sufficient to convict a defendant. But, because judges and juries want to have as much evidence as possible before convicting, often the state will introduce physical and scientific evidence in addition to the testimony of the victim and other witnesses.

THE DEFENSE CASE

When a defendant is charged with a crime, he or she may be entitled to an appointed attorney as guaranteed by the Sixth Amendment. In all cases, a defendant with the financial resources can hire an attorney. The defense attorney is present to insure that a defendant's rights are not violated, and the goal of the defense is to obtain a dismissal or acquittal whenever possible. The strategies used will vary depending on the kind of case, but will generally be as follows:

- the "evidence" is insufficient
- the state violated the defendant's rights in gathering the evidence
- the witnesses cannot be believed
- mistaken identity
- self-defense
- entrapment or involuntary act
- the defendant is unfit, insane, or guilty but mentally ill

The defense may argue that the evidence is insufficient where there is little physical evidence like fingerprints to connect the defendant to the crime, and where the witnesses may have had little opportunity to observe the defendant. Even where there is strong physical evidence, like a match between the defendant's blood and blood collected at the scene, the defendant may argue that the state violated the defendant's rights in gathering the evidence. In this kind of case, the defense may also attack the police investigation techniques, or the crime lab's processing and analyzing of the evidence.

The defense may be that the victim can't be believed. This defense is commonly seen where there are few witnesses other than the victim of the crime. The defendant attacks the motives of the victim in reporting the crime or in identifying the defendant. For example, the defendant might argue that the victim made up the story of the assault or battery to avoid getting into trouble for coming home late. Another defendant might claim that the victim wanted the insurance money for an item of property that was reported stolen.

SEXUAL ASSAULT CASES

In sexual assault cases, where the defendant is an acquaintance of the victim, he or she may admit the sexual acts, but contend that the victim agreed to have sex. This "consent" defense attacks the believability of the victim and is often used where there is a lack of evidence of bruising or other injury to the victim. If the victim is a child, the defendant in this type of case will typically argue "fabrication" by the child due to immaturity or coaching by some adult.

MISTAKEN IDENTITY

Mistaken identity is often claimed by defendants when the victim is physically injured or where the defendant is a stranger. This defense questions the victim's memory and accuracy of identification. Today, scientific improvements like fingerprinting and DNA (deoxyribonucleic acid) genetic matching techniques have made it easier to identify stranger-defendants, but the mistaken identity defense is still raised where there is a lack of scientific evidence.

SELF-DEFENSE

In bodily harm, physical assault, or battery cases, the defendant may claim self-defense. Most states require the defendant to have acted on a reasonable belief that the conduct was necessary to avoid imminent physical harm or death, but the "unreasonableness" of a defendant's belief does not seem to deter claims of self-defense. Recently, for example, an Illinois newspaper reported that when a 200 lb. man was arrested for the murder of his 110 lb. co-worker, he claimed he stabbed her to death in self-defense after she tried to "force" him to have sex in the parking garage on their way to work!

ENTRAPMENT

A defendant may also claim "entrapment" as a defense. This is common in drug cases where the defendant contends that the police enticed or lured the defendant into committing the criminal acts. Another defense, involuntariness, might be seen in gang or multiple-offender cases where the defendant argues that he or she was "forced" by the other defendants to go along and commit the crime.

THE INSANITY
DEFENSE

One of the required elements for a criminal charge is the ability to form a criminal intent. When a defendant is incapacitated, unfit, or insane, he or she may claim to have lacked the necessary mental state to commit the crime or to stand trial for committing the crime. All states have procedures for determining fitness and sanity. These hearings will require expert psychiatric evaluation and testimony, and may result in deferral of prosecution for some period of time. If such an option is not available, there may be a finding of dangerousness or insanity, and a proceeding to commit the defendant into a mental health facility for treatment until he or she is no longer dangerous or insane. Such a defendant is then subject to release under the state's mental health code.

In some states, "guilty but mentally ill" is permitted as a method of responding to some of these criminals. A finding of guilty but mentally ill permits incarcerating these offenders in mental health facilities for the duration of their mental illness, then transferring them to prison for the remainder of their sentences.

SURVIVING THE CRIMINAL JUSTICE SYSTEM

2

In the past 20 years, the National Crime Survey has recorded more than 119 million violent crimes including rape, robbery, or assault.[1] The latest National Crime Victimization Survey conducted by the U.S. Department of Justice reported that there were nearly 11 million violent crimes and 31 million property crimes committed in the U.S. in 1994. These crimes included 2.5 million aggravated assaults, more than 400,000 rapes and sexual assaults, and 23,000 homicides. While males have the highest rate of victimization, rates for males are declining, but rates for women (more than 4.7 million crimes annually) have remained constant or are increasing. Men are more likely to face victimization by a stranger; women are as likely to be attacked by an acquaintance. In addition, hundreds of thousands of children are victimized every year in the United States, usually by someone they know.

The reality is that anyone can become a victim. And being the victim of a crime is just the beginning of a long and difficult journey in the criminal justice system.

THE IMPACT OF CRIME

Not all crimes are alike, nor are all victims affected the same way by crime, but most victims do experience some sense of loss as a result of crime. Victims may have physical, emotional, and psychological injuries, as well as loss of property. Even if the crime perpetrated against you or your loved one is relatively minor from the standpoint of the legal system, it may have a profound impact on you.

Many victims report feeling powerless, fearful, guilty, confused, and angry. Realize that recovering from the crime may take some time. Short term crisis intervention will help, but it may take a year or longer to regain a sense of normalcy in your life. You may feel overwhelmed by the crime against you and may not think you have enough energy to fight for your rights, but there are ways!

GETTING HELP

There are many avenues that victims can look to for support. If you have a religious or spiritual advisor, check with him or her for resources. Sometimes a friend can offer rest, comfort, and assistance, but often friends and family members need help understanding the crime themselves and may not be able to offer much help, or may not know much about the criminal justice system. The services of a psychiatrist, psychologist, psychotherapist, or counselor may better suit your needs. The title of the helper is not as important as whether that person is competent to deal with your specific kind of case.

Make sure you ask about credentials and experience in handling cases like yours. Talk with the person and then make your decision. Meeting with a trained person who can help you make sense of what you're feeling can also help you gather the strength you need to stay and fight for your rights.

In 1984, the Federal Government passed the Victims of Crime Act, which provides funding to the states to develop and initiate programs for crime victims. Today, many states have funded programs which provide information, counseling, and advocacy to crime victims. These programs can provide you with crisis intervention through hotlines, explain financial procedures, help acquaint you with court procedures, and provide information on local shelters and centers.

VICTIM-ASSISTANCE PROGRAMS

Victim-assistance personnel act as a liaison between the victim and the criminal justice system, and their services are free of charge. Many larger police departments and prosecutor's offices employ victim-assistance, sometimes also called victim-witness, personnel. Because these programs are funded locally, they may be very thorough and comprehensive, or they may be limited to providing information only. Usually, at a minimum, these persons can help to explain local procedures and will often have local resource information for your referral.

HOTLINE SERVICES

Some public or private agencies have established "hotlines" to assist crime victims. These phone lines may operate 24-hours a day and are usually called "crisis" lines. Often, a trained staff member or volunteer can help ease your immediate concerns over the phone and set up an appointment for you to see a counselor or refer you to another resource. These hotlines may also be set up for information and referral only. Many hotlines do provide confidentiality, but before leaving any identifying information, make sure you understand what kind of confidentiality is offered by the hotline service.

CRISIS COUNSELING

Many states also provide funding for agencies to provide some counseling and peer support to victims of crime. Rape crisis centers and domestic violence shelters are a few examples. Many programs also serve the families and significant others of the victims.

Programs may offer a number of free counseling sessions for victims and significant others, or may charge according to a sliding fee scale, based on your ability to pay. The programs may also run support groups for victims to join together and talk about their situations. If you do choose a program which has a charge, remember that you may be able to file an insurance claim or seek reimbursement through your state's crime victim compensation program, so keep a record of your billing.

Many crime victims are concerned about their privacy rights when they share intimate fears and details of the crime with a counselor or in a support group. In recognition of the victim's privacy concerns, some states provide legal protection for a victim's privacy rights, and counseling programs are often available on a confidential basis. Before you choose, make sure you understand what kind of confidentiality is available through that person or agency.

THE CRIME VICTIM ADVOCATE

A crime victim's advocate is a person who can provide information, assistance, and referral services. Some can provide services immediately after the crime, such as rape advocates who go to the hospital with the victim. Advocates can be volunteers or staff members of large or small private or public agencies. Most have attended some kind of training on court systems and processes; and should be able to provide you with information on the procedures which will apply to your case.

HOW TO FIND A PROGRAM

Most nonprofit crime victim organizations obtain some state or federal funding in addition to private resources. Each state has an administrator for the federal funds, and this agency will have a listing of the programs which receive funding to provide crime victim assistance. Many private and public programs advertise or network with their local police or prosecutor, and they will be able to refer you for help.

If you have checked your local resources — police, prosecutors, the yellow pages, the library, city hall — and cannot find a local program, look for a statewide listing of victim service programs. Sometimes, a state agency or organization can provide assistance even if they are not based in your town or county. Contacting your Attorney General's Office can also be useful, since many of them have victim service information. Finally, your state representative or senator may have information to assist you in finding a local chapter of a statewide network.

WHAT IF THERE ARE NO LOCAL PROGRAMS?

Some jurisdictions have not yet established formal programs to help victims. If you have no luck in finding a program, there may nonetheless be an informal group that meets. Ask your local police officer or prosecutor for assistance in finding such a group. In Appendix D of this book you will find selected national agencies which may also be able to assist you in finding a local resource.

THE VICTIM IN THE CRIMINAL JUSTICE SYSTEM 3

Even though the crime is committed against the victim, the victim is often seen as peripheral to the case. The victim is not a party to the case, and cannot force the prosecutor to act on his or her behalf. The law does not permit a victim to privately prosecute a criminal case. For many years, victims did not have any rights. They were expected to appear and give testimony, often without much preparation from the prosecutor. It may take months, even years, for a case to come to trial, and many victims just dropped out of the criminal court process.

But victims are essential to successfully prosecuting a case, and during the 1960s and 1970s, victim's rights groups began to be heard by the criminal justice system. Eventually, every state passed laws giving victims some rights to information and participation in the case. But many times, the agencies required to provide victims rights fail to do so. As a result, most victims remain unaware of their rights to participate in the case, so they don't demand it.

FAMILY MEMBERS AND LOVED ONES

The attack on the victim will often have serious consequences for the victim's loved ones. Anger and disbelief are common feelings. When a victim is killed as a result of the crime, the family and loved ones often suffer severe emotional, and even physical, effects from the crime.

For many years, these family members and loved ones didn't have a role in the criminal justice system. In most cases, they aren't witnesses and so cannot testify. They weren't given notices of court hearings and often didn't know exactly what was happening in the case. They weren't asked how they felt to have a plea bargain struck, and they sometimes didn't even know the sentence at all. Today, this has changed and if a victim dies, the family or a designated person steps into the victim's shoes and has the rights granted to the victim in that state or jurisdiction. Thus, if your family member or loved one was killed, you become the "victim" for purposes of notification and the right to participate in the criminal justice system.

WITNESSES

Witnesses have many of the same concerns about privacy and safety that victims have, so in an effort to encourage witnesses to come forward and testify, the law has included witnesses in some of the protections given to crime victims.

THE GROWTH OF VICTIMS' RIGHTS

The first Presidential Task Force on Victims of Crime was established in the 1980s. Since then, there have been evolving improvements for crime victims.

Before the Presidential Task Force changed medical protocols, rape was not considered an injury by many hospitals. Now, rape evidence collection kits exist and the training of hospital staff has improved the experiences of the victim. These kits standardized the type and quantity of evidence collected, so that all medical procedures and evidentiary requirements could be completed in most cases at the initial emergency room visit. Also, training of medical personnel improved the understanding of the dynamics of certain kinds of crimes which resulted in more sensitive treatment of victims. For example, prior to training, some medical personnel blamed domestic violence victims for the crimes, asking "why didn't you leave, if this has happened before?" or "what were you two fighting about this time?" This made victims more reluctant to report the true nature of the injury. Some preferred to say that they had "fallen down stairs," or "bumped into a door," rather than be humiliated with questions or comments from medical staff. Training on the dynamics of domestic violence, including the cycle of violence often present in these cases, improved the treatment of the victim and made victims more likely to report the crimes.

Prior to the changes in the law, the victim's name and address were available as public records. As a result, victims were easily accessible to harassment by the media, insurance and security salesmen, and the perpetrator of the crime. Today, release of the victim's address on public records may be prohibited. Some states also provide victims with protection from the assailant's intimidation by adding new crimes for communication or harassment of a witness, and increasing penalties for offenders who harass witnesses prior to trial. In some states, the offender's bail may be revoked if he violates the condition prohibiting him from contacting the victim pending trial, and he could return to jail until trial.

After being arrested, some offenders continue to harass their victim, either from a jail phone or after being released on bail (often without the victim being made aware of the release). When releasing the accused on bail, judges weren't always aware of continued threats or harassment of the victim. Today, prosecutors more often confer with victims regarding danger issues and bail conditions. In some states, information about bail release is available, and intimidation of the victim may specifically be cause for the revocation of bail.

Prior to changes in the law, no one would tell the victim what was involved in a preliminary hearing, how long it would take, or how to prepare. Now, victims are entitled to know about the procedures. Prosecutors and victim-witness personnel take the time to prepare the victim.

In order to avoid overzealous defense investigators, the state of Oregon gives victims a constitutional right to refuse to speak with defense investigators.

Victims and assailants often came in contact with each other in the hallways surrounding the preliminary hearings, causing the victim continued distress. Victims are now entitled to wait in areas that minimize contact with the defendant.

Repeated continuances can cost the victim unnecessary expenses such as hiring a baby-sitter, leave from work, and parking. Some states require the judge to consider the impact of continuances on a victim; Ohio even permits the victim to object.

Prior to 1982, refusing to disclose your home and work address could result in being held in contempt of court. In order to maintain the privacy of the victim, some states prohibit compelling a victim to testify as to their address and other identifying information unless there is a valid legal reason.

Testifying can be a terrifying experience, especially to a child. Certain victims may now have a support person present in court; child victims may be entitled to specialized consideration.

Prosecutors could be repeatedly reassigned before the trial began. Victims would have to tell each new prosecutor the detailed story and would not receive notification of continuances. As a result of new laws, some prosecutor's offices have a single prosecutor stay with the case from start to finish in certain kinds of felonies. Victims are also entitled to information on continuances.

Because of these improvements, initiated since the 1982 task force report, victims now have some legal rights in the criminal justice system that did not exist just over a decade ago.

CONSTITUTIONAL RIGHTS OF VICTIMS

The most important right that one can hold under the criminal justice system is a constitutional right. Defendants have had them since the founding of our country, but even though the President's Task Force recommended the addition of a Crime Victim's Amendment as long ago as 1982, victim's rights are still not in the U.S. Constitution. Instead, many states have passed state constitutional amendments which grant victims the right to be treated with fairness and dignity in their state's criminal justice system. The state listings in Appendix B will tell you if the state has such a constitutional amendment or provision.

If your state has a crime victims' constitutional amendment, your next step is to get a copy. Since most amendments have been passed within the past few years, be sure to get the most current revision of your state's constitution. The Attorney General of your state will be able to supply you with a copy of your state constitution, or any public library which has a current copy of your state constitution should have a copy of the amendment. Even if your state does not yet have a constitutional provision, all states have passed laws giving crime victims some statutory rights. For more on how to find the laws of your state, see Appendix C on legal research tips, and the listing for your state in Appendix B.

VICTIM "BILL OF RIGHTS" LAWS

By 1990, every state passed victim rights laws. Most are called "bill of rights" acts. Many of the laws apply to cases prosecuted in both criminal and juvenile courts, and some states include certain specified misdemeanor and vehicular crimes. Family members or close relatives may be designated to participate on behalf of a minor, incapacitated, or deceased victim. In some states, the victim is permitted to designate another person to exercise the victim's rights. Typically, the laws provide victims with the right to information, participation, and services.

RIGHT TO
INFORMATION

Most states provide that victims are to be informed of their role, general procedures, and the medical, social, and financial services available to victims. Some states have produced form notices which police give to victims at their first contact. The victim may be provided with a name, address, and contact phone number of the police officer or prosecutor assigned to the case. Larger police departments may have victim-assistance officers who keep the victim informed as to the status of the case and provide any notices or written follow-up to the victim on victim-assistance programs, such as available crisis intervention or crime victims' compensation (sometimes called "reparation").

Although some information may be automatically provided, states commonly require the victim to request to be kept informed of case progress. Send letters to the police and prosecutor requesting to be kept informed. These letters also serve to keep officials informed of your address and other contact information. (For a sample letter to police and prosecutor, see Form A in Appendix A.) Case information may include the status of the investigation, arrest, release of the accused on bail, filing of charges (or decision not to file), commencement of prosecution, hearings and continuances, sentencing date, and judge's decision or judgment of conviction and release of the offender.

RIGHT TO
PARTICIPATION

The role of the victim in the criminal justice system is expanding, and victims are entitled to participate in criminal proceedings in virtually every state. In some states, the victim is permitted to present testimony at the bail hearing regarding fear of harm or threats by the defendant. In others, the prosecutor is required to confer or consult with the victim prior to making charging decisions.

In many states, the victim is now entitled to be present at court proceedings on the same basis as the defendant. In some states, the victim's welfare is considered in determining whether continuances will be granted, and one state (Ohio) permits the victim to object to a continuance request. A few states also permit the victim to bring a support person into court while the victim testifies.

Perhaps the most critical phase of a criminal case for the victim is the sentencing decision, and all states permit some victim input into consideration of the sentence. Because the vast majority of criminal cases are resolved by plea bargain, the sentencing hearing will be the only opportunity for the victim to speak to the judge about the crime. In many states, the prosecutor is required to consult with the victim prior to plea negotiations or agreement (this does not mean that the victim can force the prosecutor to take any particular action, but only requires the prosecutor to consider the victim's position). Also, written "victim impact statements" are often included in the materials the judge considers prior to approving a plea or determining a sentence. In some states, the victim is entitled to present the statement in person and to recommend an appropriate sentence.

Victim impact information is also crucial in consideration of parole, pardon, or commutation of an offender's sentence, and many states permit written and oral presentation of a victim impact statement to parole officials. Victims are entitled to know if the offender escapes and if he or she is recaptured. In order to exercise this right, victims must keep corrections officials informed of their address. See Form C in Appendix A for a sample letter to corrections officials.

FREEDOM FROM INTIMIDATION AND HARASSMENT

States expressly provide that victims be given information on the right to be free of intimidation while cooperating with law enforcement in the prosecution of their case. Secure or safe waiting areas are to be provided to victims while attending court proceedings to minimize their contact with the defendant and the defendant's family and friends. The police or other criminal justice personnel may provide protective assistance, and in all states, intimidation of the victim can be a criminal act. In some states, the prosecutor may specifically request revocation of the defendant's bond for intimidating, threatening, or harming the victim or the victim's family.

RETURN OF PROPERTY
Court procedures can be lengthy. Property taken as evidence or recovered by police in the possession of the offender should be "promptly" returned to the victim once its evidentiary purpose has been met. In some states, this means that once police photograph or the crime lab analyzes the materials, they should be returned to the victim. In a few states, officials are required to return property within 5-10 days after requested by the victim, unless good cause can be shown why the property cannot be returned.

THE RIGHT TO RESTITUTION

Some states make restitution mandatory, while others permit the victim to make a request for consideration by the court in the victim impact statement. For an explanation of restitution, see the section on restitution in Chapter 16.

THE RIGHT TO COMPENSATION

Every state has passed a crime victim's compensation (reparation) law which provides victims with the right to seek compensation from the state for their monetary losses incurred as a result of the crime. Each state's requirements differ. For example, in one state the victim must report the crime to police within 72 hours. In other states, the law only applies to "violent" crimes. The Attorney General's Office of each state will be able to provide you with the necessary information on how and where to file for crime victim's compensation. One warning, however, do not wait too long before investigating your rights as there are time limits within which you must file your claim. For a more detailed explanation of your rights to compensation, see the book *Victim's Rights*, by Attorney William Ginsberg (published by Sphinx Publishing, Clearwater, Florida, available through Sourcebooks, Inc).

THE RIGHT TO CIVIL JUSTICE

Every crime is a public wrong, but it is also a private wrong. Private, or "civil," wrongs are called "torts." The crime of battery, for example, is also a tort of battery. Torts are the basis for "personal injury" and "property damage" civil lawsuits. So, every crime victim is also entitled to file a civil lawsuit to seek money damages for the pain, suffering, and economic losses caused by the crime. Some states also permit victims to file civil restitution liens against the defendant, and to file claims for the offender's profits that he may make through selling the rights to his story or by writing a book or selling paintings as John Wayne Gacy did.

CASE MANAGEMENT

Criminal cases may take a long time to complete. Preparation includes organizing your materials so that you have ready access to important information which you may need as you travel through your case. You may also need this information for use in the civil case, or to check on the offender's release information. Organize material from the oldest (on the bottom or in the back) to the newest, and use folders or colored sheets to separate topics. The following suggestions will help you keep good records:

- Select a place to keep your records. Obtain a storage or moving box with a cover, a large file folder or 3-ring binder from an office supply store, or clear a space on your bookcase or in a drawer.

- Take every form, brochure, or informational sheet that is offered to you or that is available for victims of crime. Even if you are not sure that you may use the service listed, take it.

- When you are at the police station, or the hospital, ask for copies of brochures and other forms for crime victims.

- Contact your local crime victim's crisis center or resource center for information. Request that they send you any available information pertaining to your fact pattern.

- Put every sheet that pertains to crisis or emergency victim services on one file, section, or stack. You may need these hotline numbers in the middle of the night or during a crisis.

- Ask for a copy of your police report, and any other available law enforcement documents.

- Contact your local prosecutor's office or speak to victim-witness personnel for copies of charging documents and relevant laws.

- Check with your State Attorney General's Office for a victim's or crime bureau or division, and ask them to send you copies of information on crime victim compensation and other programs for victims.

- Separate police, prosecutor, and legal information into separate stacks or files.

- Keep a log for each file. Every time you have a contact write down the date, to whom you talked, and a brief description of the discussion.

- Take a notepad and pen with you when you meet with criminal justice officials and attend court proceedings. Be aware, however, that if you take notes into court with you, the defense attorney may want to examine them. Check with your prosecutor before you do so.

- Keep copies of letters you write to police, prosecutors, the judge, or corrections officials.

- Use a small calendar to keep track of events in your case. Carry it with you to all meetings and hearings, and write down any future or continuance dates.

- Use a small address book to keep the names, addresses, and phone numbers of police and prosecutors, judges, victim-assistance personnel, probation, corrections, and parole officers. Do not hesitate to request a name, address, and telephone number. Take a business card, if one is available.

Throughout your case, update your records. There is no need to keep several copies of each item; one will do. By organizing your records, you will be able to utilize information in filing insurance claims and crime victim's compensation forms, during testimony, at sentencing and parole hearings, or for filing a later civil lien or a civil suit.

YOUR PRIVACY RIGHTS 4

The criminal justice system is generally open to the public. The concept of a public proceeding promotes fairness and openness in decision making. News media often assign reporters to cover police beats and trial dockets. Many people will recall the tremendous press coverage of well-known defendants, such as O.J. Simpson and Mike Tyson. The theory is that the public has the right to know what goes on in the courts in order to guard against government abuse that could occur if secret proceedings were permitted, and that the press has a First Amendment right to obtain information and report on what goes on in the courts. But respecting the media's First Amendment rights can conflict with the profound impact that the crime has on a victim's sense of privacy, safety, and security. The public nature of criminal justice proceedings may intimidate some victims from seeking justice. Therefore, states have attempted to balance the privacy interests of victims with the openness of criminal proceedings.

PROTECTING THE VICTIM'S PRIVACY

During the 1980s, the growing victim's rights movements increased sensitivity to the issue of victim privacy. Some police routinely "blackout" identifying information from police reports. Since the press has usually obtained identifying information about the victim of a crime from police records, this can protect a victim from press scrutiny before trial. Also, some members of the press are sensitive to crime victims' privacy interests and may have an internal policy which prohibits printing a victim's name and address in certain kinds of cases, like sex crimes. (But in 1980, the United States Supreme Court decided that the First Amendment requires that in all but rare cases the criminal trial had to remain open to the public and the press.[2]) Thus, once the case is filed, court documents with victim information become available to the press.

Some states have responded by enacting legislation that would prohibit police, prosecutors, or other public officials from releasing this information to the press. Thus, private identifying victim information does not become part of the "public record." For example, Pennsylvania law provides that the victim's address and phone number shall not be disseminated to persons other than the police, prosecutor, or corrections officials without the consent of the victim.[3]

There is also some protection for victims while testifying in open court. In some states, a victim cannot be compelled to testify as to his or her address or phone number. Ohio, for example, permits a prosecutor to seek a court order to protect the victim from being compelled to provide a home address, business address, phone numbers or similar identifying information.[4]

Cameras have also invaded the courtrooms. By the end of 1991, 38 states permitted cameras in trial as well as appellate courts. In some states, only appellate courts permit cameras, but in others, like California, it is within the discretion of the trial judge to permit cameras in the courtroom. Some judges protect a victim's privacy by not permitting the cameras to show the victim's face while testifying.

YOUR RIGHTS AND THE MEDIA

The choice to speak to the media is the victim's. Sometimes reporters can become demanding, but a victim is never required to give any kind of statement to the press. On the other hand, some victims have chosen to publicize their cases in an effort to gain attention to the crime or their treatment, and media coverage can be a cathartic experience for some victims.[5] One magazine's sensitive coverage of crime victims won an award from the National Victim Center.[6] Another won a Pulitzer Prize.[7]

REPORTING THE CRIME 5

Reporting the crime to police sets the criminal justice system in motion. An immediate report to police provides the best opportunity to apprehend the offender before crucial evidence is lost or destroyed. Prompt reporting is also important in prosecution.

Some victims immediately report the crime. In other cases, a passerby, eyewitness, friend, or family member calls police. In cases of violence between acquaintances, domestic violence, rape, and child abuse, it is not unusual for the victim to wait hours, days, months, or even years before notifying police. Although the police are primarily trained to investigate current reports of crime, many departments encourage citizens to report older cases as a way of solving repeat crimes. A criminal may continue to attack victims, developing a pattern over time, but police cannot begin to recognize it as a pattern unless victims report the crimes. Even if the victim waited several years to report, if the offender has continued to commit crimes, the victim's evidence may still be used in a criminal case to establish a pattern, or for sentencing information, in another current case.

CONTACTING THE POLICE

Once you call the police, do not reenter or move about in the areas where the offender was present. These areas will become the "crime scene" and may produce evidence to convict the offender of the crime. If you have been physically injured, or there is blood or other bodily fluids on (or in) you, resist the urge to wash up. Do not change your clothes. The hospital will want to collect these items as evidence. And if you use a towel or other item to wipe the blood off, tell the police, so that it can be collected.

THE ROLE OF HOSPITALS AND MEDICAL PERSONNEL

If the victim does not report the crime to police, but instead seeks treatment at a hospital or medical facility, in certain states the hospital is required by state law to notify the police if treating a crime victim. The victim may choose to proceed with charges or not, but the police will come to the hospital.

Hospitals are a part of the criminal justice system because they can be a collector of evidence on the victim's body. For example, in a rape case, the hospital can collect hairs, fibers, semen, saliva, and blood left by the offender on the victim. In most states, this examination is free of charge, and some states have a standardized evidence collection kit. If the victim presses charges, the hospital gives the evidence directly to police.

Do not be afraid to ask medical personnel what the procedures and tests are that you are going through. Some hospitals have a crisis or social worker who can come to the emergency room to explain procedures. Others may call a crisis worker upon your request. You may not be able to understand everything, but it may help calm you to know what is happening.

If you have blood on your clothes, or other evidence of the crime, your clothes will be taken as evidence. In such a case, you will need a change of clothes. Sometimes, hospitals have sweatsuits or other clothing to give to the victim. If you are a family member or loved one, be sure to bring clothing for the victim. It can often help to regain a sense of control to have your own clothing after the emergency medical treatment.

THE POLICE INVESTIGATION 6

Police are responsible for taking crime reports, investigating, collecting evidence, and apprehending suspects. Investigation includes questioning the victim and all witnesses to the crime, and identifying, collecting, and analyzing evidence to prove the existence of the crime. Any item of information that can be used to prove an element of the crime is considered evidence.

Upon arrival on the scene, the responding officer should begin by identifying him or herself and determining what crime occurred. Police officers are now trained in "crisis intervention" techniques that are designed to increase their sensitivity to the stress of the victim. The officer will immediately determine whether emergency medical treatment is necessary and call for the appropriate assistance.

THE VICTIM INTERVIEW

The officer will question the victim to obtain preliminary information. The victim will be asked to described what happened (date, time, place, details) and to provide information concerning the defendant's identity or description. For example, the officer will want to know how the offender made contact with you. The offender may be following a pattern; he or she may be an experienced criminal who commits crimes only at certain times or in certain places.

Sometimes, the offender will "test" the victim before a robbery, mugging, or other attack. This testing can be a brief period of conversation, like asking for help or directions. It is important, if possible, for you to recall the exact words that were used. What actions did the offender engage in? The offender may have a telltale nervous habit such as a twitch or muscle tic that can help identify him or her. During the attack, it is important to remember what the offender did, said, and touched.

Finally, did the offender threaten you by telling you not to call the police, or warn you that he or she knew where you lived or worked? Sometimes, an offender will boast about other crimes he or she has committed. For example, during a robbery, the robber might say, "don't be like that other man and fight me now." Police can use that information to try to link the offender with other area crimes with similar patterns.

Police recognize that the shock of the crime may cause a victim's initial statement to be confused or disorganized. If the officer asks clarifying questions, do not assume that the officer is challenging you or doesn't believe you. He or she simply may need more details. You may not know the answer to some of the questions or remember certain details. If you don't know or can't remember, let the officer know that. Don't try to fill in the gaps with what you think or guess. At a follow-up interview you may remember more.

Police also are trained to understand that many victims may express their frustration and fears through anger, and may direct some of their anger at the officer. They don't usually take it personally.

After the responding officer has obtained preliminary information, the suspect's description will be broadcast to other officers in the area and a search for the offender will begin. The responding officer will continue to question any other witnesses to the crime.

THE CRIME SCENE

The "crime scene" is a phrase used to describe any area of the crime in which evidence might be present which helps prove the crime. A crime scene can be a car, bedroom, house, business, section of woods, trail, or any other place where the crime occurred. Police will immediately close off the crime scene so that no one except evidence technicians have access, until all potential physical evidence is collected. If the crime scene is outside, it is very important that police immediately close the area to traffic so it does not become contaminated by people moving through it.

The crime scene may contain physical evidence such as fibers, hair, stains, fingerprints, or footprints. The victim can help police identify the crime scene area by pointing out how and where the offender came into contact with the victim, the movement of the offender, and what was touched during the crime. The victim can also identify what the offender took from the crime scene upon leaving. As noted above, even the victim can be part of the "crime scene" if the attack was a personal assault.

Police will collect all items that may contain evidence and mark it for review by crime lab scientists. Crime laboratories exist in all states. The Federal Bureau of Investigation also does crime analysis. The laboratory receives the evidence and scientifically analyzes it to determine what it is and where it may have come from. For example, in a case where the victim is murdered, fibers removed from the victim's body may be identified as matching the carpet of a certain make and model of car. This evidence is then reported to the investigator on the case who may be able to link that type of car with the defendant.

THE DETECTIVE'S ROLE

If the offender is known, the police will attempt to locate and question that person. If the victim or witnesses do not know the identity of the offender, and the suspect is not immediately found from the description given, a report is completed and the case is usually turned over to a detective or investigator for follow-up.

The detective or investigator continues the investigation into the facts of the crime. This officer is usually more experienced than the patrol or responding officer, and will follow up all leads in an effort to identify and collect evidence. The detective will likely need to re-interview the victim. This time the interview will be in much greater detail in an effort to uncover additional information which might help in the investigation. If the suspect is unknown, the detective may investigate possible candidates for motives and alibis.

THE RIGHTS OF THE VICTIM

Under victim's rights laws, the victim has a right in many states to request information on the status of the investigation, and where it does not compromise the investigation, the police will usually provide that information. Although it is the practice of many police officers to routinely keep the victim informed, it is a good idea to write a letter to the detective or investigator requesting to be kept informed of the status of the investigation. (See Chapter 3 and Form A in Appendix A.)

Address the request to the police officer in charge of the investigation, usually called an investigator or detective. Usually this is the officer who will maintain contact with you to provide updates and information as the case progresses, but sometimes a victim must contact the police station to find out who has been assigned to the case. Once the name of the investigator is available, do not be afraid to call that person and ask about the case. This keeps the case on the mind of an investigator who may have several ongoing cases. After the interviews, periodically ask to meet with the investigator to talk about the case.

Because you will have a lot of unfamiliar feelings and questions, it might help if you keep a log and write down your questions and the names of the persons you have spoken to in the police department concerning your case. Also, if you remember additional details, you should write these down and contact the police promptly with this information. You may be unaware that you possess vital information, or you may remember something that the police don't know.

ARRESTING THE OFFENDER 7

IDENTIFYING THE OFFENDER

The police have a variety of methods to track down the identity of possible suspects. If the suspect is caught near the scene shortly after the crime, and the victim is able, the victim may be asked to identify the offender in a procedure called a "showup." In a showup, the suspect is "shown" to the victim for identification purposes. A showup may be on-scene, or at the police station, or the victim may be taken to the suspect by police car.

A victim may also go to the police station to look through a series of "mug" book pictures of prior offenders or to help an artist make a composite drawing in an effort to identify the suspect. Or the victim may go to the police station to attend a lineup procedure.

LINEUP PROCEDURES

Lineups can be in-person or by photos. Many victims fear in-person lineups because they think the offender can see them. In an in-person lineup, several persons matching the same general description are literally lined up with the suspect. The victim views the suspects through a one-way mirror or with some other device that permits the victim to see the individuals, while they cannot see the victim. If the suspect has been charged with a crime, he or she has a right to have an attorney present. The suspect's attorney will be permitted to observe you as you examine the lineup participants.

The police detective should first explain the procedures involved in the lineup, and keep you out of sight of the offender. Do not hesitate to ask the officer to stay near you during the identification procedure, if you feel concerned. The officer will ask you if you recognize any of the individuals, and, if so, how you know them. Take your time in looking at the lineup, and if you can identify the offender, do so clearly. This establishes the identification of the defendant as the offender without any prompting from the police.

In smaller jurisdictions where an in-person lineup is not feasible, a photo lineup may be used. Several photos are shown to the victim depicting similar looking individuals. The victim is then asked the same questions as in the in-person lineup procedure.

UNKNOWN OFFENDERS

If the victim does not know the identity of the offender and cannot spot him through the "mug" books, the police may use new scientific advances in an effort to identify the attacker. For example, DNA (deoxyribonucleic acid) is the new "fingerprint" evidence of the 90s. DNA identifies a person by his or her genes because every person's DNA is unique. If the offender leaves his DNA at the scene through blood, saliva, or semen, the police can collect it and send it to a crime lab for identification.

MAKING THE ARREST

Once sufficient information is available, if the offender can be found, police should arrest the suspect. Upon arrest, the defendant will be read his or her *Miranda*[8] rights to remain silent and to obtain an attorney. If the defendant chooses not to talk to police, they cannot continue to question him or her. If the defendant chooses to talk, any statement the defendant gives to police will be closely scrutinized later to determine whether the defendant's rights were violated and whether the statement was given voluntarily.

After the arrest, police continue to gather evidence to meet the legal elements of the case. For example, upon arrest, the offender's clothes and body are examined for possible evidence. The police will take his clothes as potential evidence. Photographs of the offender may be taken to show any identifying marks or defensive wounds the victim may have inflicted.

The police will continue to search for any property taken from the victim. For example, if the charge is based on a home invasion in which several items are stolen, the police will search for and try to recover any of the stolen property to be used as evidence in the case. All persons have a right against unreasonable search and seizure, and the police may be required to obtain search warrants from a judge in order to collect some of the evidence.

WHAT IF POLICE DON'T MAKE AN ARREST?

In any number of cases, police may not arrest a suspect. There may be insufficient evidence of all the legally required elements of the crime, or the offender may never be identified. If police do have sufficient evidence, the offender may have fled the jurisdiction or gone into hiding to evade arrest. If the police do not make an arrest once the suspect is known or the whereabouts of the suspect are known, the victim can request that the police continue the investigation as new information is uncovered. The victim should also ask to meet with the investigator to find out why an arrest hasn't been made. If the victim is not able to meet with the investigator, ask to meet with the Chief of Detectives, a Captain, or even the Chief of Police for an explanation. If the police won't arrest the suspect, the victim can go to the local prosecutor's office and seek assistance.

FILING THE CHARGE 8

WHO MAKES THE DECISION TO FILE?

Because the government must prosecute a criminal case, the final decision to pursue a state charge rests with a county or city prosecutor (also known by other names such as a district attorney, parish prosecutor, borough prosecutor, or state attorney). For Federal charges the decision rests with the U.S. Attorney's Office. For felony cases, once police have completed their investigation, the file and all reports are provided to the prosecutor's office for consideration. In some jurisdictions, for misdemeanor cases, police may recommend that charges be filed, or may file a charge if a police officer witnessed the offense. Similarly, the victim may also pursue a misdemeanor charge against a defendant by appearing before a court officer and requesting a charge be filed. In all cases the prosecutor represents the state.

SCREENING THE CASE

Prosecutors have a great deal of discretion in deciding what to charge, and the law may permit the prosecutor to choose from several different possible charges. For example, a prosecutor may choose to file a less serious misdemeanor rather than a felony in a given case. The prosecutor may also choose not to file a charge at all, usually based on one or more of the following reasons:

- reasonable doubt of the suspect's guilt

- reluctance of a key witness to testify

- cooperation of the accused in the arrest of others

- a legal element of the case is not present

- the circumstances of the crime are such that a jury is unlikely to convict

If a decision is made not to prosecute, some larger prosecutor's offices have established a review process, sometimes called "felony review." If you believe the prosecutor didn't have all the evidence or failed to consider a crucial piece of information, a review should be requested and the prosecutor should reconsider filing charges in light of the additional evidence. If the prosecutor still refuses to charge, consider contacting the head of the prosecutor's office or your state's Attorney General for assistance.

METHODS OF CHARGING

There are generally three methods by which a crime can be charged: complaint, information, and indictment. In some jurisdictions, petty offenses and less serious misdemeanors are charged by a "complaint" form. This complaint may be made by the victim or the prosecutor on a form provided by the county or municipal criminal court clerk's office.

For felony crimes, the prosecutor signs the complaint, which may be called an "information." The case then goes before a judge, at a "preliminary hearing," to determine whether there is sufficient evidence to proceed with bringing the defendant to trial. The prosecutor can also take the case before a grand jury to seek an "indictment." In some states, even if the grand jury refuses to indict, the prosecutor can still file a complaint.

THE GRAND JURY

The grand jury process may be used instead of the preliminary hearing (see Chapter 9 for an explanation of preliminary hearing) or in addition to a preliminary hearing. A grand jury is like any other jury. It is made up of citizens usually selected from the voter or motor vehicle registration lists. The grand jury determines whether charges should proceed in criminal cases brought before it.

The prosecutor presents evidence to the grand jury who will determine whether there is probable cause to charge the defendant. If the grand jury believes there is probable cause, they render a "true bill." If not, they render "no bill." (Generally, the grand jury will render a true bill because only the prosecutor presents evidence at the grand jury hearing. Therefore, the grand jury usually does not hear any evidence that tends to indicate the defendant is not guilty.) If a true bill is returned, the defendant is indicted and a warrant will be issued for his or her arrest. If no bill is returned, the case does not go forward. If the defendant has already been picked up, he or she is released.

TIME LIMITS

With the exception of murder, nearly all offenses have time limits within which the charges must be filed against the suspect. There are exceptions to the time limits, and each state varies in the limitation period it permits for charging crimes. These time limits are called "statutes of limitation," since they literally limit the time within which a charge can be brought. Even if the offense has a time limit, there are exceptions to the statutes of limitation. For example, if the suspect flees the jurisdiction before he or she can be arrested, the time period stops while the suspect is absent from the state.

SPECIAL CASES   Many states have also extended the time period for cases in which the victim is a child and for some types of sex offenses, because these crimes cause serious trauma that may keep a victim from reporting the crime to authorities for a long period of time. It may be only after the victim becomes an adult that the crime can be safely reported to police. A number of states have extended the time limit for charging this kind of case.

THE CHARGES IN YOUR CASE

To fully understand what crimes are charged in your case, obtain the exact statutory citation, which will be listed on the charges filed against the defendant. Ask your prosecutor or victim-witness coordinator to provide you with a copy of the charges. With these statutory section numbers, you can find the state's criminal code which will list the elements and the potential sentences for each crime. (See Appendix C on legal research.)

PRETRIAL PROCEDURES 9

The procedures before trial often determine the strength of the prosecution and defense case, and will narrow the issues to be raised at the trial. This is the longest part of the criminal case and can take more than a year to complete. Critics of the criminal justice system have argued that it is very painful for the victim to keep waiting for a resolution of their case, and in some jurisdictions there have been efforts to speed up the process. Nevertheless, the defendant often benefits by extending the time, hoping the victim will "give up" or maybe just move away and leave no forwarding address.

THE ROLE OF THE JUDGE

A judge presides over the criminal case. Today, most judges are attorneys with experience in criminal trials. When a legal question arises, the judge makes the decision based on the laws, procedures, and previous case decisions. He or she has a duty to remain impartial and to see that the criminal justice process is fair and just for all participants. This means that the judge should not "take sides."

If a jury has been requested, the judge oversees the selection of a jury to be sure that a "jury of the defendant's peers" is chosen. The judge will determine whether the state has enough evidence to proceed with trial, and is also the person who approves continuances. Once a jury is chosen, the judge will determine what evidence can be heard, subject to the applicable criminal law and rules of procedure. If a jury has not been requested, the trial is called a "bench trial" and the judge will decide both questions of law and fact.

All states have rules of evidence and procedure which govern the prosecutor and defense questioning of the victim and other witnesses. If one side objects to a question, it is the judge who will decide whether the witness must answer the question.

THE VICTIM'S RIGHTS

In most states, the victim has the right to know what the status of the case is prior to trial. In some states, prosecutors will automatically notify the victims of pending dates, but it is also common that the victim must request information. If your state requires that you request this information, be sure to put your request in writing. For a sample letter to the prosecutor, see Form B in Appendix A.

In many states, the victims' rights laws permit the victim to be present at court proceedings, subject to the rules of evidence, on the same basis as the defendant, or at the judge's discretion. The rules of evidence govern whether a witness can be present in court. For example, courts often allow a prosecutor or defense motion to exclude witnesses where one witness' testimony might be improperly influenced by watching another witness testify. If the defense tries to have you excluded from the proceedings, make an oral or written request to the prosecutor to permit you to stay in the courtroom. Unless the defense can show a valid reason why you should be kept out, you should be able to stay. Also, some states permit you to have a support person present in court. The same objection should be made if the defense tries to keep out that person. The judge will make the final decision on whether you can be present and under what circumstances.

Victims are entitled to be free from intimidation and harassment while attending court proceedings. A "secure or safe waiting area" may mean a separate waiting room, or waiting in the office of the prosecutor or the victim-witness coordinator, or it may mean waiting in an empty jury room or office. If no provisions have been made in advance, ask the prosecutor for assistance in directing you to a waiting area that minimizes your contact with the defendant, and the defendant's family and friends while awaiting hearings. If you or your family are harassed, threatened, or harmed at any time during the criminal proceedings, immediately notify police and the prosecutor so that appropriate action can be taken to protect you or your family.

THE RIGHT TO A SPEEDY TRIAL

The defendant has a right to a speedy trial, which is defined by law. The time period is shorter if the defendant remains in jail pending trial. The defendant can demand that the state meet the time limits and if it fails, the case will be dismissed and the defendant is released. If the state violates the defendant's speedy trial rights, the defendant cannot be retried because it would violate the Constitution. However, in many cases the defendant requests a continuance, and is required to waive his right to a speedy trial, at least for the period of delay he seeks.

Some states have provided that the victim has a right to a "speedy disposition." This right is not accorded the same weight as the defendant's rights, but it may entitle the victim to object to delay, or the prosecutor to raise the effect of continuances on victims. Some judges are becoming more sensitive to the needs of victims in determining whether to grant continuances. Violation of victim's right to a speedy disposition will not result in dismissal or release of the defendant.

ARRAIGNMENT—DEFENDANT'S INITIAL APPEARANCE

Within a short time after arrest, the accused, now called the defendant, is brought before a judge for the initial appearance, called an "arraignment." The arraignment proceeding informs the defendant of the charges and provides an opportunity for the defendant to make a plea of guilty, not guilty, or no contest. If the defendant pleads guilty, he or she admits the charges and a conviction can be entered against him or her. A not guilty plea means that the case will continue towards trial. In a no contest, or "nolo contendere," plea, the defendant does not admit anything, but agrees that the court may enter a conviction against him (nolo contendere means "I will not contest"). A no contest plea is helpful for the defendant because the facts of the case are not proven and thus cannot be used in a later civil trial as evidence of guilt. If the defendant does not answer or make a plea, it will be presumed that the plea is not guilty. At this first hearing, an attorney will be appointed for the defendant if he or she cannot afford private counsel. The defendant has a right to have the charges read, but many defendants waive this right. The defendant will likely plead "not guilty." Where bail has not been preset, the judge makes the decision to grant or deny bail to the defendant. The date for the next hearing, usually called a "preliminary hearing," will usually be scheduled at this time.

BAIL

Most defendants are eligible for release pending trial. Bail is the method by which a defendant provides money or other security to insure his or her return to court. The bond is the document that the defendant signs, which identifies what was posted (e.g., money, house, etc.) as security. In the least serious cases, pretrial release is permitted without bail, and bail is generally available to most defendants who are charged with a crime. Exceptions differ by state law, but generally certain types of murder charges are nonbailable offenses. Originally, the purpose of bail was to ensure that the defendant would return to court for the trial, and the amount set was high enough to secure the defendant's return while not being excessive which would violate his or her constitutional rights. Today, in addition to securing the defendant's appearance for trial, the protection of the public is also a consideration in setting bail.

THE BAIL HEARING

The amount of bail is preset for some crimes, so the defendant will know exactly how much he or she has to produce to gain release. If the defendant can produce bail, he or she can be released within a short time after the arrest. Many victims are shocked to see the defendant out on the street the day after being arrested.

In serious felonies, bail is not usually preset, and a bail hearing will be held to determine the amount and conditions of bail. In a bail hearing, the court will consider:

- the nature and circumstances of the crime, including whether there was force, weapons, impact on, and injuries to, the victim

- the likelihood that the prosecution may upgrade the charge to a more serious offense

- the defendant's attempts, if any, to avoid prosecution

- the defendant's ties, or lack thereof, to the community

- the defendant's prior criminal history

- the potential sentence for the offense charged

- relevant victim information

Today, the prosecutor can present evidence of the defendant's dangerousness, and the judge will consider whether the defendant is a threat to the victim, the victim's family, or the public in deciding whether to grant bail. In California, for example, the protection of the public is a primary concern in bail consideration.

Generalized fear of the defendant will not usually be sufficient, but the presence of threats by the defendant during the crime, or the actions of the defendant's family or friends in intimidating the victim should be brought to the prosecutor's attention prior to any hearing on bail so that the judge can take that into consideration when determining whether to grant bail. If the defendant has made threats against you or you have reason to fear that the defendant knows where you work or live, ask your prosecutor to request the judge to deny bail to the defendant.

If the defendant is granted bail, he or she must usually put up a "bond." In rare cases the bond is the defendant's word that he or she will return. The defendant who is permitted to sign for release is said to be released on his or her "recognizance." More likely, the defendant will have to post a monetary bond. The exact amount of the bond depends on state law, but it may be some percentage of the total amount, and it can be deposited in money, property, or other item of value. Some jurisdictions permit a defendant to post a percentage of the court-ordered bail amount. The court is entitled to an administration fee and will return the deposit if the defendant meets the conditions of bond. If the defendant does not, the full court-ordered amount is forfeited. Bail is usually higher in felonies because of the seriousness of the crime. If the defendant cannot deposit the amount required, or if bail is denied, the defendant will remain in jail while awaiting trial.

CONDITIONS OF BAIL

If the defendant is out on bail pending trial, every state has certain conditions that must be met, and additional conditions that can be required by the judge for the defendant to remain free. Mandatory conditions commonly include that the defendant:

- Appear at all court dates
- Follow all court orders
- Remain in the state pending trial
- Commit no crimes pending trial

If the prosecutor produces evidence that other conditions are necessary to protect the victim, victim's family, or the public before trial, the court can include other items, such as that the defendant:

- Possess no firearms
- Refrain from communicating to the victim or the victim's family
- Refrain from following the victim or appearing at the victim's school or work
- Refrain from alcohol or drug use
- Undergo alcohol or drug treatment
- Undergo counseling
- Get or keep a job
- Attend school
- Support his or her dependents
- Observe a curfew
- Remain in the custody of another person or agency
- Be supervised by another person or agency
- Vacate the household (if the victim is a family member)

In Utah, the victim has a right to appear before the judge to provide input on issues related to defendant's release. In most states, however, the prosecutor is charged with presenting evidence on dangerousness, so make sure to tell the prosecutor before the hearing to include as a condition of bail that the defendant stay away from your work, home, and family.

Get a copy of the court order listing the conditions of defendant's pretrial release. If you believe the defendant has violated any of the conditions, tell the prosecutor right away. Call the police if the violation is immediate, so you can get help and the violation can be recorded. When the defendant violates conditions of pretrial release, he or she can lose the right to freedom while awaiting trial.

PRELIMINARY HEARING

This hearing is usually held soon after the defendant's initial court appearance. The purpose of this hearing is to determine whether probable cause exists that a crime was committed, and that this defendant committed the crime. This hearing will be held before the judge. The police officer will testify and the victim may also be called as a witness. The defendant does not have to produce any witnesses (remember he or she has no burden of proving his or her case), but does have the right to cross-examine any prosecution witness at this hearing. After the witnesses have been presented the judge will either determine that there is sufficient evidence to continue to trial, or can dismiss the case and release the defendant.

PRE-TRIAL MOTIONS

Most criminal court cases are delayed for a considerable time period while the state and defendant investigate the case. Both the state and the defendant may request information and may file "motions" to discover information. Motions are merely oral or written requests made to a judge. Motions can involve the charges, witnesses, or evidence. Many motions will not require the victim's presence, but in some states, notice of scheduled hearings on these motions may be provided to victims. Some common motions include:

MOTION TO DISMISS

This motion can be made by the state or defendant. Sometimes the state will elect to proceed on a few of many possible charges, and so may dismiss the rest at some point prior to trial. The defendant may also ask the court to dismiss the case on the basis that the charge is defective because it fails to meet the legal requirements. A defendant may also ask the court to dismiss the case when the state failed to meet his or her speedy trial rights.

MOTION TO SUPPRESS

The defendant may make a motion to suppress the introduction of evidence of his or her arrest or identification by the victim. This motion is also made by the defendant to stop the state from using a confession or other evidence obtained in violation of the defendant's rights. For example, the defendant may argue that the confession wasn't voluntary, or he or she was denied the right to legal counsel, or that items were taken from him or her in an unreasonable search or seizure. If such a motion is granted by the judge, the state would not be able to use that confession or item of evidence against the defendant at trial. Hopefully, the other evidence against the defendant will be sufficient for a conviction.

MOTION FOR CONTINUANCE

Trials may be continued for legitimate reasons, like a delay in analyzing evidence or witness unavailability, but many cases are continued at the request of the defendant as a strategy to make the victim drop out of the case. Judges are trained to scrutinize the reasons for continuance requests. In some states special consideration must be given to the effect of a continuance on the victim. For example, in Ohio, the victim can object to a substantial delay in proceedings, and upon request, the prosecutor will file a motion with the court to consider the victim's wishes.

MOTION FOR CHANGE OF JUDGE OR VENUE

If the judge is prejudiced or if, for example, pretrial publicity is so biased that the defendant cannot get a fair trial, these motions may be filed seeking to change the judge or move the trial.

MOTIONS FOR DISCOVERY

These very common motions are often searches for evidence. Most motions relate to the identification, analysis, or production of forensic or scientific evidence. Some motions may involve questions surrounding identification and qualification of expert witnesses.

With regard to discovering information concerning the victim, states apply differing approaches. Victims may generally refuse to speak to, or to be interviewed by, the defendant or defense investigators. In some states, however, the victim may be required or ordered to attend a deposition to give a statement before a court reporter under oath. In others, depositions are not permitted in criminal court. To protect its victims, an Arizona constitutional amendment provides that victims may refuse interviews, depositions, or other discovery requests.

PLEA BARGAINING 10

Plea bargaining has existed in some form in the United States since the early 1800s. Today, it is not unusual for some jurisdictions to resolve 80–90% of their felony cases by plea bargain. It is called a "bargain" because both the state and the defendant derive some benefit by the deal. The state does not have to risk a trial and the possibility of losing (and the defendant gets at least some punishment and a criminal record); the defendant does not have to risk a longer or more severe sentence. The judge must still approve of the agreement before it can be entered in the court. A judge can also reject a plea bargain.

TYPES OF PLEA BARGAINS

There are two major types of plea bargains. In the first type, the defendant negotiates away certain charges so that only a lesser charge (or charges) remain pending. For example, if a defendant is facing two charges—a home invasion with a possible sentence of 6–30 years and burglary with a possible sentence of 3–7 years—by pleading guilty to the burglary in exchange for dismissing the home invasion, the defendant has reduced his potential sentence to a maximum of 7 years (instead of 30).

The second type involves an agreement by the state and defendant to a particular sentence in exchange for a guilty plea. In the above example, the state and defendant would agree that the prosecutor would ask for no more than 15 years on the home invasion (rather than the 30 possible), and 3 years on the burglary (rather than 7).

PROCEDURES

Commonly, plea negotiations take place very early in a case. In this way, the defendant "tests" the confidence of the prosecutor to see how strong the state thinks its case is, or the state may "test" the defendant to see how readily the case can be disposed. For example, if the prosecutor feels the evidence is weak or a victim is wavering, the state may readily agree to a plea bargain. Similarly, if the defendant is not confident of his or her ability to win at trial, but can arrange a lesser sentence or a reduced charge, the defendant may be willing to plead guilty. The earlier the offer, the more likely it will be generous, but a plea bargain may be reached at any time, even in the middle of the trial.

The defendant has certain constitutional rights in making a plea, and the plea must be voluntary. Therefore, even if the judge approves of the agreement, there will be a short hearing before a court reporter in which the defendant will be questioned as to his or her understanding of the plea.

THE VICTIM'S ROLE

Because of the critical impact that a plea bargain has on the victim, states now permit or require prosecutors to confer or consult with victims before an agreement is made. Some states require prosecutors to consider the victim's concerns prior to engaging in plea negotiations (these are currently Arizona, Illinois, Kentucky, Montana, New Hampshire, Ohio, Pennsylvania, South Carolina, South Dakota, and

West Virginia). At least one state (Maine) requires the prosecutor to state the victim's wishes in court before an agreement is approved by a judge.

To include victim impact information, some states require the victim to prepare a victim impact statement. See the section in Chapter 13 on "Sentencing—Victim Impact Statement" for details on what should be included in such a statement.

THE CRIMINAL TRIAL 11

If the defendant does not plead guilty, the case will go to trial. The Federal Constitution requires the government to follow certain rules before a person can be convicted of a crime, and this has led to the passage of many laws protecting a defendant's rights. The prosecution of a criminal case is an adversary process, which means that both sides can present evidence to prove the guilt or innocence of the defendant.

DEFENDANT'S RIGHT TO A JURY

The trial may be by jury in serious criminal cases. Sometimes, it is the defendant's strategy to demand a jury, because in most states, the verdict of the jury must be unanimous to convict. If the defendant can convince even one juror not to vote for conviction, then no guilty verdict will be entered against him or her. In some cases, the defendant may choose to waive a jury trial, and the case is tried by the judge and is called a "bench" trial.

Each state has adopted procedures for jury selection. Random pools of jurors are picked to appear and answer the questions of a judge or the attorneys in a questioning process called "voir dire" (pronounced "vwa dear"). The questions determine whether a proposed juror is qualified to serve on a particular jury and to identify grounds for removal. Once a jury has been selected, the trial is ready to begin.

OPENING STATEMENT

The trial begins with an overview of the case, called an "opening statement," given by each party or its attorney. The state has the entire burden of proving the case, so it goes first. The prosecutor outlines the theory of the case and what he or she believes the witnesses, and any other evidence, will prove to the jury (or to the judge in a bench trial).

The defense also has the right to make an opening statement, which will sometimes be given right after the prosecutor's opening statement, and sometimes be given just before the defense attorney begins presenting his or her evidence. The defense attorney may wish to delay his or her opening statement until the prosecution has finished presenting all of its evidence. This is because it may be difficult for the defense attorney to decide what witnesses he or she will call until the prosecution's evidence has been heard and seen. If the prosecution has not presented a good case, the defense attorney may decide that he or she does not need to present any testimony (since the prosecutor has the burden of proof, and the defendant is innocent until proven guilty beyond a reasonable doubt and cannot be required to testify).

EVIDENCE AND TESTIMONY

All of the information that can be considered by a judge or jury in a criminal trial is presented through witness testimony and by introducing documents, physical items, and scientific evidence. Each state has rules which govern the admissibility of evidence, and not all information that is relevant will be permitted to be introduced into the trial. For example, information that is highly prejudicial to the defendant, like a long-past criminal conviction, is weighed against its importance to the current case before it can be admitted. One notable exception is California which constitutionally provides for "truth in evidence" in criminal trials. California's constitution provides that "relevant evidence shall not be excluded" in juvenile or criminal offenses except under specified circumstances. (Art. I §28 (d))

Most of the preliminary motions have determined what evidence will be permitted at trial, but some questions may arise during trial. Objections may be raised by either the state or defendant for many reasons. The judge must then decide the matter before the trial continues.

Each side will present witnesses by "direct" examination. The questions will be asked first by the attorney who is sponsoring the witness, followed by cross-examination by the opposing attorney. For example, a prosecution witness might be the police officer. The prosecutor asks questions on direct examination of the officer, which is followed by cross-examination by the defense.

The purpose of direct examination is to tell the story, to find out what happened, so the questions will be open-ended and allow the witness to explain the event. An example follows:

Prosecutor:	"State your name and occupation."
Police Officer:	"John Doe. I am a police officer with the Gotham City Police Department."
Prosecutor:	"Do you recall the night of January 1, 1996?"
Police Officer:	"Yes."
Prosecutor:	"Tell the court what happened on that night."
Police Officer:	"I was on duty that night, and at approximately 12:10 a.m., while driving my patrol car at the corner of Elm and Fifth Street, I observed a woman on the curb waiving her arm at me."

The purpose of cross-examination is to limit or test the witness' recollection of the event, or to show that the witness has not told the entire story or is lying, in an attempt to undermine his or her credibility and reduce the impact of the testimony in the case. Cross-examination can also be used to show the bias, interest, or motive of the witness. The questions are designed to lead the witness to a particular answer.

Police are often attacked in a criminal case by the defense as a strategy to undermine the evidence against the defendant. The defense attorney in the example above has checked the police roster for January 2nd, and found that the police officer was not on duty that day. He also noticed that the date on the officer's police report is January 6th. This led to the following exchange on cross-examination:

Defense Attorney:	"Isn't it a fact you were *not* on duty that night?"
Police Officer:	"No. I was on duty until 11:55 p.m., and was on my way home in my patrol car when I first saw Ms. Smith."
Defense Attorney:	"Isn't it true that you didn't even complete your police report until several days later?"
Police Officer:	"Yes. I didn't complete my report until I could speak with a particular witness again."
Defense Attorney:	"So you don't really remember that night, do you?"
Police Officer:	"I remember that night very clearly."

Here, the defense attorney's attempt to discredit the officer was not very successful, but you should get the idea of the difference between the tone of direct examination and cross-examination.

THE STATE'S CASE

Because the state goes first, it chooses the order in which the state's witnesses will testify. Depending on the type of case, and an evaluation of available evidence, the prosecutor may have the victim testify first, but may also call other witnesses to "set the stage" for the victim's later testimony. Common witnesses include police officers who investigated the case, evidence and lab technicians who collected and analyzed the evidence, eyewitnesses, and experts who can assist the judge or jury in understanding the evidence to be presented.

THE VICTIM AS A WITNESS

PREPARATION
FOR COURT

The victim may be the state's primary witness in the case, and will usually be required to testify at trial. You have likely waited a long time for this day. Now that it has come, you are likely to be nervous and maybe frightened. You may have experienced testifying at the preliminary hearing or at some other pretrial motion, but that was some time ago. The emotions experienced during the crime can be rekindled at the court hearings. For example, anger, fear, and hatred may interfere with your ability to tell the story. Today, you will be confronting the offender in court. The defendant's family and friends may also be in the courtroom watching you. The best way to overcome these fears is to be prepared.

Preparation by the prosecutor will help you, but you should also make an attempt to familiarize yourself with court procedures. If possible, make a visit to other courtrooms to watch testimony in unrelated cases. Sometimes victim-witness personnel in the prosecutor's office can set up a time to tour the courtroom in which you will likely testify. Even cable or "court-TV" documentary programs may help you visualize the court process. Watch carefully the demeanor of the witnesses who testify and especially become aware of the role of the defense attorney and of the strategies used in defending cases.

TESTIFYING IN COURT

A victim's demeanor in testifying is very important. Sometimes, in an effort to be calm and controlled, the jury may think the victim is too unemotional to be "genuine." But if the victim is too relaxed, the defense attorney may use that fact against him or her.

In preparing you to testify, the prosecutor will likely suggest that you:

- Tell the truth.

- Do not volunteer information.

- Do not use drugs or alcohol to calm nerves.

- Do not memorize testimony.

- Be straightforward and speak clearly.

- Say so, if you are unsure of the question.

- Look at the judge or jury when answering a question.

- Listen carefully to each question before answering.

- Dress conservatively.

- Understand that the goal of the defense attorney is to discredit you.

- If a question cannot be answered with a yes or no, say so, or explain that you must give two answers to the two-part question.

- Do not guess at answering. If you don't know the answer, say "I don't know."

- If you are interrupted before you finish your answer, ask if you can finish your first answer to the first question before answering a new question.

- Objections: Both the prosecutor and defense attorney will object. If so, stop talking and wait for the judge to rule.

- Do not follow the commands or instructions of the defense attorney; only the judge can issue orders.

- Do not argue with the defense attorney.

- Control your anger.

If it seems like that is a lot to remember—it is. But, just do your best. You know what happened, so tell it as best you can to the judge and jury. You are not in control of all the rules and procedures, but you are in control of yourself.

THE DEFENSE CASE

After the state completes its case, the defendant is entitled to introduce his or her evidence through the same methods. The defendant may introduce alibi witnesses or witnesses who attack the evidence offered by the state. In criminal cases, however, the defendant has a constitutional right not to testify and the state may not suggest any reason for the defendant's failure to testify. The state has the same right as the defendant to cross-examine the defense witnesses.

CLOSING STATEMENT

After each side has completed its case, the state and defendant summarize their cases through closing arguments. The state will argue that the case has been proved beyond a reasonable doubt and will likely remind the judge or jury of each important witness' testimony. The defendant will argue that the state failed to prove that the defendant committed the crime beyond a reasonable doubt. The defendant may also attack the state's witnesses as being unreliable or having a motive to lie, and therefore suggest that the evidence was false or improperly used against him or her. Once the defendant completes closing argument, the state will usually have one more chance to convince the judge or jury that the evidence was sufficient to convict the defendant.

THE VERDICT 12

THE ROLE OF THE JURY

Once both sides have completed their presentation of evidence and testimony, the case moves to deliberation on a verdict. There are a range of possible verdicts in most states, including guilty, guilty but mentally ill, not guilty, and not guilty by reason of insanity. Contrary to what you may hear from members of the news media, "innocent" is not available as either a plea or a verdict. In freeing a defendant, all a jury determines is that the state did not prove guilt; not that the defendant proved innocence. The guilty verdicts permit the entry of a judgment of conviction and permit a sentence to be imposed on the defendant. The not guilty verdicts do not permit either conviction or a sentence.

Not guilty by reason of insanity developed from the concept that the law should not hold a person criminally accountable for actions over which he or she has no control. If a person lacks the ability to control his or her actions due to mental illness, then that person is not to be blamed and should not be punished for these actions. States differ on the standards and degrees to which the defense of insanity will be permitted. A person found not guilty by reason of insanity is usually released (unless someone begins a civil court proceeding to have the defendant committed to a mental institution as being a danger to himself or herself, or others).

Because of public outrage over some defendants' attempts to use an insanity defense (and thereby get released), some states have adopted a verdict of guilty but mentally ill. If the jurors believe that the defendant did commit the illegal act, but has a mental illness, they may render a verdict of guilty but mentally ill. This verdict keeps the defendant in custody, and merely influences where the sentence is served. Upon conviction, the defendant undergoes a psychiatric evaluation to determine the nature and extent of mental illness, then the defendant is sent to a mental health facility to serve his or her sentence and receive treatment. If the defendant regains mental health during the period of the sentence, he or she is transferred to prison for the remainder of the term.

In a jury trial, the judge instructs the jury on the law to be applied in its deliberation, and then the case goes to the jury. The jury's job is to determine whether the facts produced at trial fit the crimes charged against the defendant, and whether they believe beyond a reasonable doubt that the defendant committed the crimes charged. If the jury believes that the state has proved its case, then it will find the defendant guilty. In most states, the verdict must be unanimous, and this applies to both guilty and not guilty verdicts. Once the jury has reached a verdict, the judge will enter the judgment of conviction. Contrary to popular belief, most jury trials result in the conviction of the defendant on at least one charge.

When a jury is unable to agree on a verdict, it is called a "hung jury" and the judge will declare a "mistrial." The state will have another opportunity (if it chooses) to try the defendant again. If the jury agrees that the evidence presented did not prove beyond a reasonable doubt that the defendant is guilty, the jury can render a verdict of not guilty. In this case, the state cannot retry the defendant again because to do so would violate the Constitutional protection against "double jeopardy" (i.e., being tried twice for the same crime).

THE BENCH TRIAL

If it has been a bench trial, (i.e., tried without a jury), then the judge "takes the case under advisement" and deliberates on the facts presented by the state and the defendant. After some consideration of the facts and the law, the judge renders a verdict in the case.

A VERDICT ON SOME OF THE CHARGES

The prosecutor may have charged several offenses for the acts committed by the defendant. The proof at trial may have convinced a jury that the defendant was guilty of only one or some of the charges, and a finding of guilt would be made on only those charges.

Sometimes, the defendant is found guilty of a "lesser included offense," which means that the defendant committed a crime, but not the highest offense charged. For example, the defendant is charged with murder which requires proving that the defendant: (1) killed the victim, and (2) did so with the intent to cause death. The jury believes that the defendant did kill the victim, but that the defendant only intended to frighten the victim, not to kill him or her. Because the law requires both elements for a finding of guilt on the murder charge, but only one is present, the jury may find the defendant guilty of a lesser-included-offense such as manslaughter (defined as the unintentional killing of a person).

THE SENTENCE 13

Sentencing generally serves three purposes: punishment, deterrence, and rehabilitation. Federal sentencing guidelines apply to federal cases, and each state has the right to design its sentencing scheme. States may follow an "indeterminate" sentencing scheme in which the judge sentences the defendant to a range of years, but the parole board may release the defendant after a certain period of time. For example, if the judge sentences a defendant to three years to life, the parole board can release the defendant upon a showing of rehabilitation even if the offender has not yet served the minimum length of time. In a determinate scheme, the range of sentence is established by state law and the judge may sentence the defendant within that range. Parole is not available for defendants in a "determinate" sentencing scheme, so that a defendant would be sentenced for a set period, for example, ten years, and would be required by law to serve a minimum set portion of that sentence.

SENTENCING DISPOSITIONS

Every state has a specific sentencing code which sets forth the range of sentence dispositions for each crime. Some states permit the death penalty for certain types of murder; other states permit up to life in prison. Many states are adopting "truth in sentencing" laws which increase the time served by repeat offenders, and "three strikes and you're out" laws which require life imprisonment for a "career" criminal upon the third conviction.

Most states permit a range of penalties for the same class of crime. For example, a home invasion and a criminal sexual assault may fall within the same offense classification, with the same potential sentencing range. Generally, the following dispositions exist (these are explained in more detail below):

- Execution (in some states)
- Imprisonment (including periodic, "boot camp," etc.)
- Probation (possibly with home confinement, electronic monitoring, etc.)
- Supervision
- Restitution
- Fine

EXECUTION
The most serious penalty available is the death penalty. A number of states permit this punishment after a conviction of its highest class of murder, or murder with special circumstances.

IMPRISONMENT
A jail or prison sentence may be mandatory for certain crimes. The maximum length of term is for the defendant's natural life, but some states provide for an indefinite term (1 to 100 years), while others require a definite term (299 years) to be imposed. Some states permit an extended term for "exceptionally brutal or heinous behavior," or for repeat offenders. States may also permit or require sentences to be imposed concurrently (at the same time) or consecutively (one after the other) if necessary to protect the public. Offenders sentenced to prison will be in the custody of the state's department of corrections which determines what prison the offender is sent to and whether the offender is transferred.

In recent years, "boot camps" have become popular for certain types of offenders. Boot camps are also called "impact incarceration." They have eligibility requirements and many states exclude the most serious crimes or repeat offenders from the program. Boot camps usually last four to six months and require physical training and labor.

Periodic imprisonment means that the offender will be released during some portion of the sentence and will be confined during the remainder. For example, an offender might spend weekends in jail, but continue to work and support his or her family during the week. Alternatively, a court may sentence the offender to spend one weekend per month in jail for the duration of the sentence imposed.

PROBATION

Crimes that include probation as an option tend to be less serious offenses. The possible length of probation varies with the crime charged. A sentence of probation means that the offender is convicted of the crime, but is permitted to remain in the community subject to certain conditions. Probation may also include some term of periodic imprisonment or community service as part of the sentence. Even if the crime permits probation, a judge can refuse to grant it if the judge believes that the crime charged requires some length of incarceration.

California and several other states have experimented with a program of probation commonly called "intensive probation supervision." This type of program is usually designed for offenders who need closer monitoring than the average probationer. It usually involves electronic home confinement which permits an offender to leave home only for specified reasons such as to attend school or counseling.

Conditions of probation usually include that the offender:

- not commit any crime
- report to a probation officer
- not possess a dangerous weapon
- not leave the state without the court's permission
- not associate with other convicted people

In addition, the court can impose other conditions on the offender, and some states require a court to impose certain conditions based on the offense. For example, in a child sexual abuse case where the offender is the father of the victim, a judge who awards probation to the offender may also order the offender to pay for the counseling or other expenses of the victim, or to pay for support of the victim during the length of probation.

Courts often require the defendant to obtain some kind of counseling in domestic violence cases. Many courts order the defendant to have no contact with the victim during the period of probation. Some may require the defendant to obtain drug or alcohol treatment, and to refrain from taking alcohol or illegal drugs.

SUPERVISION

For minor offenses, where the defendant pleads guilty or stipulates to the facts, the court may order supervision for a period of time, usually a few months, and defer further proceedings in the case. If the defendant serves the period of supervision without committing another offense, the proceedings will be dismissed and no conviction will be entered. You may also hear this referred to as "withheld adjudication."

RESTITUTION

Restitution is ordering the defendant to pay the victim for his or her economic losses. The consideration of ordering restitution is a requirement in some states, and is available whether the defendant is incarcerated or on probation. Even where restitution is not mandatory, the judge can consider restitution for the victim's losses. The victim's request for restitution should be made in the victim impact statement. In a few states, restitution is enforceable as a civil lien or judgment. Although restitution typically does not cover the complete range of claims a crime victim may have as a result of the victimization, by enforcing a civil lien or judgment the victim can proceed with collection immediately after the criminal case, rather than having to begin the process again through the civil courts. Thus, this might be pursued to avoid having to file a civil suit.

FINES   All courts can order the defendant to pay a fine as a condition of probation, and many fines are mandatorily imposed. Court costs are also chargeable to the offender.

THE SENTENCING HEARING

Unless it is a minor case, or the sentence has been the subject of a plea bargain, the sentencing decision will be made after a sentencing hearing at which witnesses can present evidence. After the verdict has been entered, the judge will usually continue the case for a few weeks for a "presentence investigation" to be completed, and for the state and defendant to prepare evidence as to what they believe the appropriate sentence should be. To determine what sentence to impose, the judge weighs several factors, including the severity of the crime and the defendant's criminal history. The court also weighs the harm suffered by the victim.

Special rules for sentencing hearings allow the judge to consider more information as "evidence" than would have been permitted in the trial, such as testimony or letters from any person who has information about the defendant's character, previous history or record of crimes, or any other information that is relevant to the issue of sentencing. For example, past victims of a serial rapist can testify at the sentencing hearing to show the defendant's dangerous nature and past criminal history, where they would not be allowed to testify at the trial.

THE PRESENTENCE   A presentence report, usually prepared by a probation or parole agency,
REPORT   helps the court to consider several factors prior to imposing its sentence. For example, if the crime permits a sentence of probation, the presentence investigation would identify whether the defendant is an appropriate candidate, or whether special conditions should be imposed. Among other information, a presentence report can include victim impact information.

THE VICTIM IMPACT STATEMENT

Victims in all states have the right to provide information to the court, for consideration in sentencing, on how the crime has affected them. A formal Victim Impact Statement may be the only time that the victim is able to speak to the judge about what has happened to him or her as a result of the crime. Where the victim has died as a result of the crime, or is a minor or incapacitated, it may be the only time that the court hears what impact the crime has had upon the victim's survivors.

In some states this information can be provided to the judge directly; in others, it must be written in a "victim impact statement" and made part of the presentence investigation provided to the court prior to sentencing. The victim may also be able to present the information orally at the sentencing hearing.

PREPARING THE VICTIM IMPACT STATEMENT

Some states require the victim to prepare the victim impact statement in conjunction with the prosecutor. If the victim is unable to present it in person, it may be able to be presented in writing by the prosecutor at the hearing. If the victim is a young child, the parents of the child may be able to prepare the statement. The statement lists the financial, social, psychological, and physical impact on the victim for consideration by the court. Your prosecutor or victim-witness assistant may have a form for you to use, but if not, the information in the outline beginning on the following page should be included. (For a sample victim impact statement form, see Form D in Appendix A.)

Victim Impact Statement

I.   Victim Information:
       Name
       Age
       Phone
       Address
       City, State
       Work address, City, State

II.   Crime Information:
       Offense
       Date
       Offender(s)
       Victim(s)

III.   Physical Injuries: [attach documentation]
       Medical
       Emergency Treatment
       Hospitalization
       Doctor(s)
       Hospital(s)
       Treatment
       Future Impairment
                Amount of Medical Expenses:
                $_____ (To Date:_____)
                $_____(Anticipated)

IV.   Psychological Injuries:
       Psychiatric Care
       Psychological Care
       Hospitalization
       Counseling
       Future Therapy
                Amount of Counseling/Therapy Expenses:
                $_____(To Date:_____)
                $_____(Anticipated)

V.   How Crime has Affected Victim and Family:
       Emotional Injury
       Change Life-style
       Change in Attitude
       Change in Family/Social Relationships
       Hardships Endured as a Result of this Crime
       Feelings About the Criminal Justice Process
       Feelings About Your Role in the Case

VI.   Employment-Related Loss:
       Ability to Earn a Living
       Loss of Job
       Loss of Wages
       Loss of Days
       Anticipated Future Loss
               Amount of Employment Expenses:
               $_____(To Date:_____)
               $_____(Anticipated)

VII.   Property-Related Loss:
       Description of Property
       Damages of Loss
       Cost to Repair, Replace
               Amount of Property Loss:
               $_____ (To Date:_____)
               $_____ (Anticipated)

VII.   Other Loss:
       Description of other Damages or Loss
               Amount of Loss:
               $_____(To Date:_____)
               $_____(Anticipated)

VIII. Sentence Recommendation:

IX.   Other Information for the Court to Consider:

PRESENTING A
VICTIM IMPACT
STATEMENT IN
COURT

In addition to preparing a victim impact statement, many states allow the victim or victim's representative to present the statement in court at the sentencing hearing. In such cases, the statement is treated like other evidence, and the defendant is entitled to cross-examine the victim at the hearing.

WHAT TO
EXPECT

The hearing will be like a mini-trial, except that it should be concluded in a much shorter time period. In most cases, a single appearance in court will be sufficient to complete the process, but sometimes the hearing will have to be continued if all of the information that the judge must consider prior to making the decision has not been gathered.

WHAT THE SENTENCE REALLY MEANS

Be aware that despite the "truth in sentencing" reforms sweeping through the country, often the prison sentence handed out by the judge isn't exactly what the offender will actually serve. Over the years, time off for "good behavior" has become a standard, and an offender will usually serve only part of the actual sentence imposed if he or she behaves while in prison.

Another problem occurs when the offender is sent back to the community to a "half-way" house or with electronic home confinement. This prisoner may still be considered to be "in-custody" even though he or she is back in the community and you may be shocked because you were never notified.

Make sure that you have contact with the prosecutor after the sentence is imposed, to get an explanation in clear terms as to what the sentence really means. Find out what office or department will monitor the defendant during the sentence. Get the name, telephone number, and address of the supervising official from the prosecutor.

VIOLATIONS OF SENTENCING ORDERS

An offender who violates his sentence of probation, conditional discharge, or parole can be subject to a possible loss of freedom. For example, if the offender was ordered to stay away from the victim as a condition of probation, but follows the victim, the offender is in violation of his or her release conditions. Notify the police immediately, and request the prosecutor to charge the offender with the violation.

Once the violation is reported, the prosecutor can schedule a revocation hearing. If he has not been arrested for the violation, the offender is served with a summons or subpoena to appear in court. At the hearing, the state must show that the defendant violated a condition of his or her probation in order for the judge to revoke or modify the probation. Failure to pay a restitution order or fine is not usually grounds for revocation of probation, unless the offender willfully refuses to pay.

APPEAL 14

WHO CAN APPEAL?

In most criminal cases, the defendant appeals. If the defendant is found guilty, the defendant will often appeal. The prosecution has a limited right to appeal. For example, if the jury acquits the defendant, the defendant's right to avoid double jeopardy—being tried twice for the same crime—means the state cannot appeal.

WHAT HAPPENS TO THE OFFENDER DURING AN APPEAL?

Although the defendant may have a right to appeal, he or she does not have the same "right" to be free as prior to trial. The defendant may petition the court for release pending appeal, however, and the state will fight this request. In rare cases, a trial judge (or appeals court) may permit the defendant to be free pending the appeals court decision. If so, the same bail conditions may be required, or additional ones can be added pending the outcome of the decision. Once again, if the defendant violates the conditions of his or her release, loss of freedom may be the result. Make sure you contact the police and your prosecutor to get a copy of the release bond which lists the conditions of bail, and contact the police if you believe the defendant has violated those conditions.

WHAT CAN AN APPEALS COURT DO?

Every state has a system of courts designed to hear appeals. No testimony is taken in the appellate process, instead the appeals court simply reviews what happened in the trial to determine if a serious legal error was made. If a serious legal error was made, the conviction can be overturned and the case sent back for a retrial. If a constitutional error was made or if the error cannot be remedied, the conviction may be overturned and the case dismissed. An appeals court can also uphold a conviction, but change the sentence. Appeals are very common in criminal trials, but reversals are rare.

THE VICTIM'S RIGHTS

Victims in many states can request to be informed that an appeal has been filed, and of the status of the appeal. The Attorney General's Office or a state or local appeals prosecutor will defend the appeal, and the victim can request information from that office. If an appeal includes oral argument, it is a public hearing at which the victim has a right to attend. If you do not know who to contact regarding the appeal, start with the prosecutor or victim-witness assistant who will have (or can find) information for you. Make sure you get a name and contact information to follow-up on the appeals process which can take several months to a year, or even more.

AFTER THE CRIMINAL TRIAL 15

WHEN IT'S OVER

As you have likely discovered through your journey in the criminal justice system, you are not alone in experiencing the many intense emotions of a victim. Once your case is over, though, you have become a survivor and you can become a resource to others who are just beginning to face this bewildering process.

Contact your local, state, or federal politicians to register your opinion on current legislation or proposals. Contact the media to keep them informed on issues which continue beyond your case. For example, if you were not afforded your rights under the crime victim's rights laws, contact a local newspaper about improving the process for others. If your offender is about to be released back into the community, you can write a letter to your local newspaper or state representative.

Investigate your community and join an organization to speak out for other victims. Become a support person for another victim. Volunteer court-appointed special advocates may be needed by your juvenile or criminal court system to speak for child victims. Some victims have even become activists and have founded organizations dedicated to improving victim's rights. Much remains to be done before victims can truly feel that the system was more just than criminal. Find your strength, and your voice, and use them.

RELEASE OR ESCAPE OF THE OFFENDER

The release or escape of a prisoner is of special concern to the victim. Although escape creates an emergency situation which cannot be predicted, the majority of release situations are determined by early release policies of parole boards and corrections officials. The Governor of each state also has the power to commute a prisoner's sentence or pardon a prisoner.

In some states, the offender is eligible for parole, but the trend is to require more offenders to serve a pre-determined length of sentence prior to release. Even if the sentence is preset, "day-for-day good time" permits most prisoners to serve only part of the sentence imposed.

Recently, states have begun enacting registration and notification laws, primarily for sex offenders. By 1995, at least 40 states enacted sex offender registration laws.[9] Under these schemes, offenders are required to register with authorities upon release, and the public, including victims, can be notified. Some states are enacting "predator" laws for repeat offenders who have not been rehabilitated. These laws permit incarceration for an additional period after the sentence is completed to protect the public.

FINDING OUT ABOUT THE RELEASE

Many states permit the victim some information on the prisoner's status. In most cases, the victim must specifically request this information and provide the appropriate corrections officials with a current address and phone number to receive this information. Write a letter to the department of corrections or parole board requesting to be kept informed of any procedures which may affect the prisoner's status, including release or transfer for work or furlough. See Form C in Appendix A for a sample letter.

PRESENTING A
VICTIM IMPACT
STATEMENT

Some states permit the victim to provide a victim impact statement or appear at the parole hearing to object to the release. This right is especially important, because the parole board does not hear the same evidence and testimony as the trial judge in making its decision. Be sure to update your victim impact statement prepared at the sentencing hearing with how the crime has continued to affect your life and the lives of your family and loved ones. The victim's impact statement and testimony may be very compelling, and public opinion has shaped the willingness of parole officials to grant early release of prisoners.

Recovering Damages 16

Criminal vs. Civil Court

The world of civil suits is completely different from the criminal justice system. The rules and procedures may sound similar, but they operate very differently in civil court. For example, the parties in the criminal case are the State, represented by the prosecutor, on behalf of the victim and all of the people in that state; and the defendant represented by his or her attorney or appointed counsel if he or she cannot afford an attorney. The victim is merely a witness in criminal court, but in filing a civil suit, the victim is in control. The parties in a civil suit are the plaintiff (victim), who may be represented by an attorney, and the defendant (the offender or a third party), who may also be represented by counsel. As a party, the victim can make all the decisions that the prosecutor could make in the criminal case. Because a civil suit is a private action, no attorneys will be appointed. If either party wants an attorney, they must hire their own counsel.

STANDARD OF PROOF

One difference between criminal and civil cases is the standard of proof required for the judge or jury to find against the defendant. In the civil case, the plaintiff must prove, usually by a "preponderance of the evidence" that the defendant caused the injuries for which the plaintiff is entitled to damages. In the criminal case, the prosecutor must prove "beyond a reasonable doubt" that the offender committed the crime for which he or she is charged. These standards are general concepts, not precise definitions, but the criminal standard is much higher and harder to meet than the civil standard. The civil standard of a preponderance of the evidence has been described as requiring the jury to find that the plaintiff's version of the facts is slightly more likely than the defendant's version. It has also been described as requiring the plaintiff to prove his or her case by slightly more than a 50% certainty.

Although it is difficult to compare the two standards in terms of a percentage, it has been said that it requires at least a 75% certainty, because some states allow convictions based upon the agreement of nine out of twelve jurors. Jurors are often instructed by the judge that if they are to find the defendant not guilty, they should have a doubt that is based upon logic and reason. A juror can have some doubt, and still convict. The standard is not beyond *all* doubt, or beyond *a shadow* of a doubt.

COMPELLING THE
DEFENDANT'S
TESTIMONY

Further, there is no right of the defendant to avoid the witness stand in civil court as he or she could do in criminal court. So the plaintiff can require the defendant to testify, and may be able to ask those questions that couldn't be asked of the defendant in criminal court.

PUNISHMENT VS.
COMPENSATION

While the focus of the criminal case is concerned with punishing the offender and deterring the offender from committing further crimes, it is not concerned with the victim's individual welfare. The victim may have lost time off of work, have pain and suffering, and may even have lost a house or job while trying to seek justice in the criminal case. The focus of the civil case is to compensate the victim/plaintiff. The plaintiff in a civil suit can find out about the assets of the defendant and literally take away the profits that the defendant may have made on the crime.

The chart on the following page shows some of the differences between the criminal and civil systems.

Comparison of Criminal and Civil Court Systems

	CIVIL	CRIMINAL
Parties	Victim=Plaintiff v. Defendant=Criminal or Third Party	State v. Defendant
Goal of the Case	Compensate Plaintiff; punish Defendant monetarily	Rehabilitate, punish & deter Defendant
Who Benefits	Plaintiff	People or society at large
Standard of Proof	Preponderance of the evidence (more likely than not)	Beyond a reasonable doubt (highest standard required)
Evidence	Inquiry very broad; Defendant generally must answer Plaintiff's questions	Defendant has Constitutional right not to testify or answer questions
Verdicts	In favor of Plaintiff, or in favor of Defendant	Guilty; Not guilty; Guilty but insane; Mistrial
Judgment	Compensate Plaintiff for losses, and punish Defendant monetarily	Defendant is punished through a sentence
Outcomes	Judgment for Plaintiff and punish Defendant monetarily; no damages awarded	Defendant sentenced to prison, jail, probation; pays restitution to victim, or fine to State
Settlement	Plaintiff chooses when and for how much	Prosecutor chooses to negotiate; Victim cannot prevent settlement

OTHER OPTIONS FOR RECOVERY OF DAMAGES

CRIME VICTIM
COMPENSATION

All states have set up a fund to compensate victims of crime. Each state sets out eligibility requirements and generally requires that victims report promptly, cooperate with the police and file a claim within a certain period of time. In addition to a civil suit, a victim should seek an award of compensation from the state crime victim's compensation fund. In most states, eligible victims can be compensated for out-of-pocket losses resulting from the crime. Where a victim later recovers damages in the civil suit, state law may require that the victim's compensation program be reimbursed from the civil damage award.[10]

RESTITUTION AND
REPARATION

As part of the criminal sentence, the offender may be ordered to pay "restitution," sometimes called "reparation." Although these terms do differ slightly, they generally reach the same result.[11] Usually, restitution is ordered for those offenders who receive probation, but some states mandate restitution be ordered regardless of the type of sentence imposed. This remedy is limited to those offenders who have the ability to pay and usually to actual out-of-pocket losses suffered by the victim. An order of restitution does not affect the victim's right to file a civil suit, but may be deducted from the recovery awarded.

INSURANCE

Insurance may cover some of the losses. For example, auto insurance will cover theft or criminal damage to a vehicle and its contents, while homeowners insurance provides similar coverage for loss to contents in the home. Medical insurance may reimburse the victim for medical and hospital expenses for injuries resulting from the crime.

The What and Who of a Civil Lawsuit

17

What is a Civil Suit?

A civil suit is a lawsuit brought by one party against another. When a person is victimized by a crime, that person has the right to file a civil suit to seek damages for the crime. In a civil action, the goal is to compensate the victim; in some cases, the suit may also result in punishing the wrongdoer.

Advantages (and Disadvantages) of a Civil Suit. In the civil case, the plaintiff chooses who to sue and for what reason. The plaintiff can decide to settle the case, and the amount that he or she is willing to accept for a settlement. But a civil suit is not quick. Even simple civil suits may take upwards of a year to complete; some can take as long as four years. Nor is a civil suit judgment an automatic award of money. The judgment is written on a piece of paper, but if the defendant is "judgment proof," (i.e., he or she is indigent, has no assets, or has hidden his or her assets well), then collecting the judgment may be impossible. In some cases, the defendant may be in jail for a long time, so the judgment may have to be held and renewed in the event the defendant inherits, wins, or earns sufficient assets to pay the damages.

WHO ARE THE PARTIES TO THE SUIT?

THE PLAINTIFF

The plaintiff is the person who files the suit. Generally, the plaintiff, as the directly injured party, will be the crime victim. Other plaintiffs can include the victim's spouse, parents, or other family members who have suffered certain losses as a result of the crime. If the victim dies during the commission of the crime or as a result of the crime, then the plaintiffs might be his or her estate and surviving family members, who will usually be able to seek recovery for the "wrongful death" of the victim.

THE DEFENDANT

The plaintiff may have several choices of defendant in a civil suit. Choosing the defendant (or defendants) requires consideration of the goals of the lawsuit. Of course, the obvious defendant is the criminal offender. However, if the criminal is never caught or has no assets with which to pay damages, then filing a suit against the offender will not result in funds to compensate the victim's losses. If a third party is a possible defendant, it may have sufficient assets or insurance coverage to adequately compensate the plaintiff's losses.

The Offender. The plaintiff may seek damages from the offender. The civil suit may be filed regardless of whether the offender has been charged in criminal court.

Multiple Offenders. If the conduct of two or more persons caused the injury, the victim can sue any one, or all of them. For example, joint liability may exist where only one of the assailants slashes the tires on the victim's car, while the others helped to drive or acted as lookouts. Each wrongdoer may be held liable for the entire damage award.

Juvenile Offenders. Generally, children under seven years of age can be held liable for intentional acts which form the basis of the criminal charge (but not for negligent acts). Even if the minor is not charged, a civil case may still be filed on the intentional act, but it may be limited depending upon the age of the child, and whether the conduct was reckless or negligent instead of intentional. Between the ages of seven and fourteen, a child can be found liable for negligence, but the jury will measure his or her conduct be special standards (i.e., experience, age, and mental capacity). Mentally incompetent persons are viewed similarly to children over age seven.

FAMILY MEMBERS
If the criminal act was an intentional act committed by a spouse or other family member, a lawsuit against the family member is generally allowed. This is not true for reckless or negligent acts, as some states will not permit such suits, based on the doctrine of "intra-familial" or "intra-spousal" immunity (the purpose of this doctrine is to maintain good relations in families, and to prevent family members from getting together on a scheme to obtain money from their insurance carrier).

THIRD PARTIES
In addition to criminal charges, a lawsuit may also be filed against any person, agency, organization, corporation, or other entity that allowed the injury to occur through negligence or willful and wanton misconduct. Today, it is common in crime victim litigation to see a third party as a defendant. For example, an employer who fails to use reasonable care in screening, supervising, or retaining a school bus driver who molests a child on the bus, may be held liable for creating the condition which led to the child's injuries. Or an apartment complex owner may be held liable to a rape victim for failing to provide adequate parking lot lighting or security.

WHAT IF THE DEFENDANT SUES THE VICTIM?

While the criminal case is pending, the criminal may file suit against the victim in an effort to intimidate the victim into dropping criminal charges. Although the defendant may have the right to file a case, all states have laws which protect victims from intimidation by the defendant. Make sure that you notify the prosecutor immediately of any attempt to intimidate you. The criminal can face new charges based on intimidation of a witness. If the case has been completed, the offender may still harass the victim by filing suit after he or she is convicted and sent to prison. Courts understand the attempts to intimidate and harass victims and while some cases are successful, nearly all reported cases have been dismissed upon request of the victim.

THE BURDEN OF PROOF

The plaintiff has the burden to prove all the elements of the lawsuit, but because this is a civil case, the burden of proof is not as strict as the "beyond a reasonable doubt" of the criminal case. In a civil case, the burden is said to be a "preponderance of the evidence," which means there is enough evidence to make it more likely than not that the defendant did the things he or she is said to have done. If so, the plaintiff has sufficiently met the burden of proof.

THE ELEMENTS OF A CIVIL SUIT

Generally, for intentional torts, the plaintiff must prove: (1) an act; (2) causation; and (3) damages. The term "intent" in an intentional tort does not mean an intent to do harm. It simply requires an intent to commit a certain act for which it is foreseeable that certain consequences are likely to occur.

Because a battery is an intentional tort, the defendant must intend to commit the act which causes harm or offense to the plaintiff. Damages are available for physical injuries as well as emotional injuries. The plaintiff may seek recovery for medical bills, lost income and earning capacity, pain and suffering, and any permanent physical or mental injuries.

THEORIES

When a crime victim files a civil suit seeking damages for personal injury or damage to property, the basis for the lawsuit is found in tort law. A "tort" is committed when one, through his or her wrongful conduct, injures another. In other words, just as a crime is a public wrong, a tort is a private wrong. For every crime there is a tort remedy against the criminal for the injured victim. Most cases allege several theories and seek recovery on as many bases as the facts will support.

Tort law is broader than criminal law. In addition to the intentional criminal conduct of the offender, any person or organization that failed to meet its responsibilities to the victim may also be held liable for the victim's injuries. The duty is usually said to be one of "reasonable care," or something a reasonable person would or would not do under the circumstances. Duties can be imposed by a state law, municipal ordinance, administrative regulation, industry standard, or even through the common practices and procedures developed throughout the years. For example, a landlord who is required by local ordinance to keep the property free of dangerous hazards has a duty to meet that standard for the tenants of the building. If the landlord fails to provide adequate lighting on the property, which permits the criminal to hide out, stalk and injure the victim, the landlord may be held liable for contributing to the condition that caused the injury.

THEORIES
AGAINST THE
OFFENDER

Most cases against the offender allege his or her intentional conduct as the basis for the suit. There are numerous legal theories which are available to crime victims. These include: assault (threats), battery (physical injury), false imprisonment (detention of the victim), property damage, trespass, theft, intentional infliction of emotional distress, rape, sexual assault, and wrongful death. If the offender is a professional or an employer, there are several additional bases to support the suit, such as malpractice. Further, if the offender is a parent, parental negligence may be added.

Assault, for example, includes apprehension, fear, and intimidation as the basis for the assault case. So, when the defendant raises his or her hand to strike, but stops short, an assault is committed even where there is no contact. And pointing a gun at the victim (even though the victim didn't know it was unloaded) would constitute an assault. However, words alone are not usually sufficient for an assault, unless some other circumstances exist that create a reasonable apprehension of immediate physical contact.

Battery is a very common element of many crime victims' civil suits. This includes a whole range of physical contact, from mere touching to severe violence, and includes both direct and indirect contact. Kicking the victim is a battery, and so is kicking away the victim's cane, because physical contact was indirectly made with the victim.

Interference with the victim's property can also be the subject of a civil suit. This includes vandalism, trespass, or damaging or destroying property.

THEORIES
AGAINST THIRD
PARTIES
If a third party had a special relationship with the victim, there may be additional theories based on negligence, including parental negligence, professional malpractice, failure to maintain the premises, or negligence in hiring or retaining an employee. For example, an employer who fails to complete a legally mandated background criminal history check on a new daycare center worker with a prior criminal conviction for molesting children, may be responsible to the child and the parents of the child who had a right to expect the employer to follow the law.

Each civil lawsuit has a number of required elements which must be proven in order to be successful. The crime victim who files a civil lawsuit is treated no differently than any other plaintiff who comes before a civil court. Knowledge of these basic elements is essential to understanding the documents which must be prepared and filed prior to presenting the case to the court.

CAUSATION

THE OFFENDER
The injury must have been caused by the action or inaction of the defendant. In the case of the criminal as the defendant, there is usually no problem in demonstrating that "but for" the acts of the criminal, the victim would not have suffered injury. A judgment of conviction on the

criminal charges proving the defendant guilty of the crime (or crimes) can be sufficient to establish the causation element in the civil case. A plea of guilty may also be admissible as evidence of guilt in the civil case.

THIRD PARTIES   Most third party defendants argue, however, that they did not cause the injury to the victim. Their argument is that the criminal's acts were not under their control. And it is true that there is no duty on the part of a third party to control the criminal acts of another. Courts, however, recognize that there can be more than one cause of injury. For example, the landlord who fails to change the locks on an apartment and allows an assailant easy access to the victim's apartment through the use of an old key, is responsible because the landlord had a special relationship with the victim tenant and failed to take action (change the locks) which contributed to the ability of the criminal to cause the victim's harm.

Often courts use a "foreseeability" test to determine whether a third party, like the landlord, could have foreseen the likelihood of the crime against the victim. For example, courts may consider whether there were other crimes committed in the apartment complex or whether another tenant complained to the management of similar criminal activities which provided notice to the landlord that these criminal acts were likely to occur.

COMMON DEFENSES

The defense of a civil suit will focus on three areas:

1. jurisdiction
2. parties
3. facts

JURISDICTION   A jurisdictional defense may be made when the case is filed in the wrong court, filed beyond the permitted time period, or where the minimum damage requests have not been made. For example, if state law permits the victim to file the suit in the county either where the crime occurred or where the defendant lives, but the victim files in another county, the suit may be dismissed for improper jurisdiction. Also, if the suit is filed on the basis of the victim's personal injury, the state law may limit the period within which a suit may be filed to a few years. A suit filed after that time would be subject to the defense that the court does not have jurisdiction over a suit filed after the permitted limitations period. Finally, some courts have damage request thresholds that must be met by including it in the initial pleading documents filed with the court. For example, suppose the state law provided that, to file in the circuit court, the complaint must seek damages of at least $50,000 (otherwise it must be filed in county district court). A complaint which requests $40,000 would be subject to dismissal on the basis that it did not meet the jurisdictional requirements of the court.

PARTIES

A defense based on the parties will usually be made by a third party defendant. In this defense, the defendant will ask the court to dismiss the case because the complaint fails to properly identify or name the defendant. For example, if the victim lists in the complaint the individual property manager, but the landlord is actually a corporation, the defendant will be improperly named. Some defendants are protected from suit by special statutes. For example, if the defendant is a governmental entity, it may argue that it is protected from suit by special laws granting it immunity.

FACTUAL DEFENSES

The defendant may argue that the victim provoked the defendant or he or she may argue self defense and try to "put the victim on trial."

Beyond the technical defenses listed above, defendants commonly raise factual defenses. The defendant may argue that the victim contributed to his or her own injuries. If the defendant is the offender and the case involves his or her intentional criminal conduct, then this defense fails, but if the facts support it, the negligent defendant may argue that the victim "contributed" to causing the injuries, in an effort to reduce a damage award on the basis of the victim's fault. For example, if the victim failed to take proper care to reasonably protect him or herself from harm, that may be considered in the civil suit. In one case, the judgment award for negligence against the owner of the premises was reduced by 97% upon a finding that the plaintiff, a rape victim, was also negligent when she opened her door to strangers without determining who was there.[12]

DAMAGES

The concept of "damages" is very broad in the civil law. In tort law, each individual is presumed to intend all the natural and probable consequences of his or her deliberate acts, but the specific result need not be foreseeable. For example, if the victim has a heart attack during a robbery, the criminal/defendant could be held liable even though he or she could not foresee the death or additional injury to the victim.

An award of damages may be compensatory, punitive, or both. The amount of money to award is a question of fact for the jury or judge. The plaintiff can request a certain amount but the jury or judge may award a greater or lesser amount.

COMPENSATORY
DAMAGES

Compensatory damages compensate the victim for tangible losses. Compensatory damages provide recovery for physical injury and resulting medical expenses, earning capacity, and pain and suffering. The proof of damages is simple in the case of medical expenses, or bills to repair or replace property, where the victim can show an exact dollar amount of loss. Determining how to put a dollar amount on past and future "pain and suffering" is more challenging. Nonetheless, these "intangibles" can be itemized, and juries and judges make awards every day which include pain and suffering for victims.

PUNITIVE
DAMAGES

Punitive damages may also be awarded to punish the offender or to deter others from engaging in the conduct that led to the offense. Punitive damages are usually awarded only for outrageous or egregious conduct. For intentional conduct, punitive damages may be appropriate. A particular statute may permit punitive damage awards in certain cases. In negligence cases, where the conduct is willful and wanton so as to "offend the sensibilities" of the public, punitive damages may be awarded. The jury may make a specific award separate from the compensatory damage award.

THE EFFECT OF THE CRIMINAL CASE ON THE CIVIL SUIT

The filing of a civil suit is not dependent on the status of any criminal proceeding. Therefore, the victim can sue at the same time as the criminal case is proceeding; and can also sue if no criminal charges are filed, or if the defendant is not convicted. If the criminal is convicted, evidence of the defendant's guilt can be used in the civil case. Because the burden of proof is higher in a criminal case, more than enough evidence of the criminal's guilt has already been proved in the criminal court. Also, a plea of guilty is admissible in the civil case. In some states, a guilty plea or conviction will establish liability and the only remaining questions will be proof of damages. In others, the defendant will be permitted to explain the reasons for a guilty plea.

Even if the defendant is found not guilty in the criminal case, it will not prevent the victim from filing a civil suit. Because the burden of proof is higher in the criminal case, there may nonetheless be a "preponderance of the evidence" which would meet the level of proof required for the civil case. In other words, although the evidence wasn't quite enough for proof beyond a reasonable doubt in the criminal case, it may be enough for the lower standard of proof on a preponderance of the evidence in the civil case. So, an acquittal cannot be used as evidence in the later civil case because it doesn't prove that the defendant didn't commit the crime. For example, the families of Ron Goldman and Nicole Brown filed civil suits against O.J. Simpson, even though he was found not guilty of their murders in the criminal case. The jury verdict in the criminal case is simply that the prosecutor failed to prove

Simpson's guilt beyond a reasonable doubt; not that Simpson proved himself innocent. Therefore, the Goldmans and Browns were still able to prove their civil case on a preponderance of the evidence.

THE EFFECT OF A CIVIL SUIT ON THE VICTIM

Now that you understand the "what" of civil suits, and you are considering your options, be aware of the impact that a civil suit may have on you. Before undertaking what may take years to complete, consider why you want to file and what resolution you would like to see. If you have access to a therapist, discuss your consideration and its potential impact on your health and well-being. Realize that the civil suit will continue the litigation started in the criminal case, and that you may not be able to put the crime behind you for some time to come. Realize, too, that there will be a financial commitment on your part as well as an emotional one. Consider carefully your willingness to "go the distance" in seeking justice. Also weigh the possibility that you may not win or collect money damages. If, upon weighing all these factors, you determine to proceed, then commit yourself to the battle and seek the justice you are entitled to in the civil court arena.

During the pendency of the civil suit, be aware of the physical and psychological effect that it has on your well-being. Numerous agencies can offer support and assistance to crime victims. Contact the National Victim Center for more detailed information on services in your locality (see Appendix D for resource information).

The How and When of a Civil Lawsuit

18

A civil suit filed in any court follows a set of procedural laws and rules which guide the process for the parties to the suit. Federal courts follow the Federal Rules of Civil Procedure. Similarly, each state has its own code of civil procedures and court rules. The parties to a civil suit must follow the procedural rules of the jurisdiction in which the lawsuit is filed in order to proceed with the case. If the lawsuit is a simple one seeking a small amount of damages, all jurisdictions have special "small claims" courts in which plaintiffs may sue, in many cases without a lawyer. If the suit is more complex or seeks a larger damage award, a different set of rules will likely apply. See Appendices B and C for guidance in finding the civil rules of your jurisdiction.

Evaluating and Preparing the Case

Careful preparation is required prior to filing a civil case.

IDENTIFYING AND COLLECTING PROOF

Identification of the proof necessary to successfully prove the claim depends on the facts of the case. What facts does the plaintiff need to prove? What crime was committed against you? Who was at fault for the crime? Who contributed to the circumstances that led up to the crime? What facts exist to prove the crime was committed? What injuries have you suffered as a result of the crime (e.g., financial, emotional, and physical)? How do you find that information? Who can provide information about your case?

Assume your apartment has been burglarized. You call the police and make a report. The burglar is never apprehended, but you learn through the police investigation that several other tenants have made similar "break-in" reports, and in each instance, the burglar gained access through the broken lock on the back lobby door of the building. Although there have been several similar crimes committed and complaints have been made to the landlord, the landlord has failed to remedy the situation by fixing the door or changing the lock. Through the police investigation on your report, you learn that your burglar also used the broken back lobby door to gain entrance to the building.

In speaking to the police, you may identify several potential witnesses to similar crimes, and you may have learned that the landlord was "on notice" and has failed to take action. Local ordinances or state laws may list certain obligations of the landlord to tenants. For example, perhaps the landlord was required to install deadbolt locks on the outer doors, but has never done so.

Although the property you lost is never recovered, you have a list of the items taken and you have valued those items. You also find that you are unable to sleep at night for fear that the burglar may return again while you are in the apartment. The crime has caused you to experience nightmares and you seek the help of a therapist. Cooperation with the police has caused you to lose days at work and you are forced to use vacation days to cover your losses.

The proof of a civil case will be offered by the plaintiff to support the facts listed in the complaint. Proof may exist in the form of the testimony of a witness or a document which includes information on an element of the civil case.

For example, proof of the commission of the crime may include information gathered by law enforcement personnel. When the police arrived at the scene of the crime, a police report will be completed listing the nature of the call, any witnesses present, any physical evidence of a crime (such as a broken window or pry marks on the door). Often there will also be supplemental reports which investigators or other law enforcement personnel may complete upon speaking to the witnesses or collecting items of proof from the crime scene.

During the prosecution of the criminal case, there will be testimony of witnesses, and the introduction of physical evidence. Most states' victim's rights laws permit the victim to obtain the prompt return of evidence collected from the victim for purposes of criminal prosecution at the end of the case. Usually, however, the victim must make this request. (See Appendix B.)

Proof of the judgment of conviction can be obtained through the clerk of the court in which the criminal conviction was entered. A copy which is certified by the court clerk will usually be required by the civil court.

To prove damages, the plaintiff may use medical or mental health records which document the physical and psychological injuries suffered as a result of the crime. The victim may also use employment records to show lost income, lost benefits, or even loss of a job due to the crime. These records can often be obtained through a written request, or the plaintiff may request a subpoena be issued, ordering the medical, mental health, or employer to release information in its files.

ORGANIZING THE FACTS
Keeping your facts organized for easy and ready reference is essential in preparing your case. Keep a diary of events from the commission of the crime, listing who you have talked to and what information you have learned, as well as your emotional, physical, and psychological reactions to the crime. If your case is prosecuted, keep a record of the events in the criminal case. Keep all of the bills you incur as a result of the crime.

THE TIME AND PLACE TO FILE

Careful consideration of the proper time to file is also crucial, as all jurisdictions place time limits on access to civil courts. In determining the best time to file suit, the victim should consider that, while the criminal case is pending, the defendant could assert his 5th Amendment privilege not to testify in the civil case. Once the defendant is convicted or acquitted of the crime, he or she can no longer assert this privilege in the civil case, and therefore can be required to testify and produce evidence. Further, because the conviction may be useful to the victim in a civil suit, the victim will likely be questioned during the criminal case about whether a civil suit is pending, to try to show the victim's motive or bias. Also, the criminal investigation may yield important information for the civil case, at no cost to the victim. For these reasons, victims may choose to wait until the completion of the criminal case before filing a civil suit.

STATUTES OF LIMITATION

Although the victim may have some choices to make about when to file the civil suit, all states provide a limitation period within which a personal injury or property loss action must be filed. The laws vary from state to state, but many statutes of limitation allow only one or two years within which to file a lawsuit for personal injuries resulting from the crime.[13] California, for example, permits a victim to file a civil suit up to one year after a criminal conviction is entered for a felony crime.[14]

Suits against particular kinds of defendants, like governmental entities, may also have special time limits or notice requirements which are much shorter than the general time limits. Check with the agency directly for any notice or form required to be filed, or check with an attorney familiar with lawsuits against governmental entities. And, although states vary, child victims generally have until they reach the age of majority within which to file a lawsuit. One new trend in child victim cases is that a number of states have recently extended the statute of limitations for adults who were sexually abused as children. See Chapter 20 for a more detailed explanation of these suits.

WHERE TO FILE

The choice of where to file the lawsuit will depend on the nature of the case, and the convenience of the plaintiff. The great majority of civil suits are filed in state courts. Often, state rules permit the plaintiff to file for injuries in the court where the crime occurred, or where the plaintiff or defendant reside.

The plaintiff may also be able to file the case in federal court under certain circumstances. The requirements for filing civil cases in federal court can be found in the United States Code Service (USCS) reporters. For example, a civil lawsuit may be filed in federal court if the plaintiff can assert claims based on the U.S. Constitution or seeks damages for violation of civil rights (see 28 USCS §1340). The suit may also be filed in federal court if the plaintiff requests damages in excess of $50,000, and the defendant resides in a different state from the plaintiff (see 28 USCS §1332). In a few cases, the suit must be filed in federal court, such as where the defendant is an employee of the federal government and the crime occurred while the employee was acting within the scope of his office or employment (see 28 USCS §1346).

The decision as to proper jurisdiction may be a clear one, but it may also be a very important cross-road in the case. If you are unsure, or your research points to options between state and federal court filings, you would be wise to consult with an attorney who has experience in the type of suit to be filed.

OVERVIEW OF THE CIVIL COURT PROCESS 19

The advent of "Court TV" and other television programs, and media coverage designed to increase public awareness of the legal system, has helped to demystify the court process for many people. The legal system is merely a formalized setting for resolving certain kinds of wrongs which fall into two broad categories—criminal and civil. The "system" is really made up of a number of independent agencies all working together as components of the process. For example, documents are filed with the county, local, or municipal clerk's office, and service of official papers is usually conducted by the local sheriff or other designated law enforcement official. Attorneys in the civil process are in private practice, although in rare cases they may be on the staff of a public agency not affiliated with the court system. The judge presides over cases assigned by the court system to a particular docket, call, or courtroom. The bailiff keeps order and security in the court. Certain other persons, like official court reporters, prepare transcripts and provide copies of evidence filed with the court.

STARTING THE PROCESS

To file a lawsuit requires preparation of certain documents which include specific information so that a court can determine what happened and what you are requesting of what defendant. For small claims court, the county or municipal clerk's office will usually have forms that have "fill-in-the-blank" sections. For more complex cases, court rules specify the format of the "complaint." Check with the local clerk's office to determine whether form complaints and other court documents are available. Some clerks or private legal supply stores may even have forms on computer disk.

THE COMPLAINT
While the procedures of each state may vary, generally an initial "complaint" will be filed by, or on behalf of, the plaintiff. All complaints include a "caption," which is a heading that includes the names of the plaintiff and defendant, the name of the court where the complaint will be filed, and a number which is assigned by the clerk of the court. Some jurisdictions require the complaint to specify the type of case being filed, (e.g., "personal injury," "tort," or "small claims").

The sample complaint that follows is not intended to represent the requirements of any particular jurisdiction, but generally provides a representation of the format of a personal injury complaint. This hypothetical case is based on the robbery of a hotel guest in the elevator of the hotel; the complaint is filed against the hotel.

A sample caption follows:

IN THE CIRCUIT COURT OF _____Cook_____ COUNTY

STATE OF _____Illinois_____

JOHN DOE, PLAINTIFF,	)))	
v.	)	Case No. _98-12345_
	)	
H. JOHNSON, INC., DEFENDANT.	))	

Victim Privacy. The complaint must include the names and addresses of the parties. Ordinarily, the filing of a civil complaint is a public record filed with the clerk of the court and available for inspection by any member of the public. Victims may be fearful of filing and thus disclosing private information. Some state laws do protect the privacy of the plaintiff victim by permitting the complaint to be filed anonymously, or by using a fictitious name or pseudonym rather than the plaintiff's name and address. An example of pseudonym filing follows:

PARTIES

    1.   Plaintiff, John Doe, is a citizen of the State of Illinois, residing at 123 Main Street, Chicago, Illinois.

    2.   Defendant, Harry Johnson, Inc., operates a hotel and is registered as an Illinois Corporation with its principal place of business at 123 President Street, Chicago, Illinois.

Jurisdiction. The complaint must also include a statement that the court in which the complaint is filed has proper jurisdiction to hear the case. In some cases the statement may include the fact that the parties reside in different states or that the amount sought is within the court's jurisdiction to hear. In some courts the claim cannot exceed a certain amount (e.g., $15,000) while in others it must exceed a certain amount (e.g., $50,000) For example:

JURISDICTION

    3.   Jurisdiction is premised upon the diversity of citizenship of the parties under the United States Code.

    4.   The amount in controversy exceeds, exclusive of interest and costs, the sum of $25,000.00 Dollars.

Facts. The complaint must include the facts on which the case is brought.

FACTS

5. Plaintiff arrived in Illinois on (date). Upon his arrival Plaintiff became the hotel guest of Defendant.

6. Plaintiff, preparing for his departure from Defendant Hotel, withdrew cash and jewelry from the hotel safety deposit box.

7. Upon leaving the registration desk where the safe deposit boxes were located, Plaintiff proceeded to the elevator lobby, and entered an elevator in Defendant's Hotel.

8. Immediately after the doors of the elevator closed, the other individual in the elevator placed a pistol in Plaintiff's back and ordered him not to move. The individual then removed, from Plaintiff's person, cash in the amount of $275.00 Dollars and the above-referenced jewelry, valued in excess of $1,280.00 Dollars.

9. When the door of the elevator opened, the assailant struck Plaintiff with his pistol using great force on the head, rendering Plaintiff unconscious. The assailant then pushed Plaintiff out of the elevator into the hallway, causing Plaintiff to suffer abrasions and contusions.

10. Upon regaining consciousness, Plaintiff returned to the main floor of the hotel to report the robbery to the security personnel of Defendant. After making a statement to the police, Plaintiff was taken to the Medical Center for medical treatment and subsequently released.

11. As a result of the assault and battery, Plaintiff has suffered severe mental anguish. Plaintiff suffers from severe headaches, has been unable to sleep, and suffers from nightmares.

12. The assault and battery has left, and will leave, a permanent scar and damage upon Plaintiff's life.

Legal Duty and Liability. The complaint must also include sufficient information to establish the duty owed by the defendant and the other elements of the tort:

13. At the time of the assault, battery, and robbery of Plaintiff, Defendant knew, or in the exercise of a high degree of care should have known, of other similar assaults, batteries and robberies, on or near its premises, or the possibility thereof.

14. At the time of the assault, battery, and robbery of Plaintiff, it was the duty of Defendant to exercise a high degree of care to maintain the premises in which Plaintiffs were invited guests in a safe condition, taking all necessary and reasonable steps to safeguard Plaintiffs from assault, battery and robbery on its premises.

15. Notwithstanding the above Defendant carelessly and negligently discharged its duties to Plaintiffs so that the above-described assault, battery, and robbery of Plaintiff occurred.

16. The negligence of Defendant consisted of the following:

(a) Failing to take proper measures to protect Plaintiff from assault and robbery after having knowledge or notice that such criminal acts were likely to occur.

(b) Failing to provide for adequate security service throughout the Hotel.

(c) Failing to warn Plaintiff of the fact of prior assaults and robberies in the Hotel, and that similar acts could occur in the future.

(d) Being otherwise negligent under the circumstances.

Request for Relief. Finally, the complaint must include a request for relief:

---

17. That Defendant's negligence, and that of its agents and employees is the direct and proximate cause of the assault and battery upon Plaintiff and robbery of cash and jewelry from him valued in excess of $1550.00 Dollars, for which Plaintiff claims compensatory and punitive damages.

Wherefore, Plaintiff John Doe request that judgment be entered against Defendant in the amount of $500,000 Dollars, together with interest, costs, and attorney's fees.

_____

[John Doe SIGNATURE]

_____

Notary Seal

THE SUMMONS

A "summons" is simply a notice to the defendant that a case has been filed naming him or her as a defendant. The summons is usually "served" on the defendant along with a copy of the complaint, by the local sheriff's office or another "process server." The summons typically includes information as to the deadline for filing a formal response, and where to file the response, and where to mail or deliver a copy of the response to the plaintiff. The exact form of the summons is usually provided for in the laws of the state, and can often be obtained from the court clerk. Most form summonses are similar to the format on the following page:

IN THE CIRCUIT COURT OF ____Cook____ COUNTY

STATE OF _____Illinois_____

JOHN DOE,	)
PLAINTIFF,	)
v.	) Case No. ____98-12345____
H. JOHNSON, INC.,	)
DEFENDANT.	)

SUMMONS

TO: H. Johnson, Inc., *(name of defendant)*

You are hereby summoned and required to file with the Clerk the above court and serve on Plaintiff/Plaintiff's attorney whose name and address are

    John Smith, Esq. 123 Main St., Any State   an answer to the complaint which is hereby served upon you, within 30 days of the date of service. If you fail to do so a judgment by default may be taken against you for the relief demanded in the complaint.

Sealed this _____ day of _____, 19 ___.

                           CLERK OF THE CIRCUIT COURT

_____

Notary Seal

THE DEFENDANT'S
ANSWER

Once the defendant is properly served with a "summons" giving him or her notice of the lawsuit, the defendant will be given an opportunity to file an "answer" to the complaint. In the answer, the defendant can admit or deny the charges and raise any defenses he or she may have. As a practical matter, the answer will not usually give you much valuable information. On the following page is an example of a typical answer.

IN THE CIRCUIT COURT OF COOK COUNTY

STATE OF ILLINOIS

JOHN DOE,	)
PLAINTIFF	)
v.	) Case No. 98-12345
H. JOHNSON, INC.,	)
DEFENDANT.	)

ANSWER TO COMPLAINT

The Defendant, H. JOHNSON, INC., hereby Answers the Complaint in the above-entitled case as follows:

1. Plaintiff's complaint fails to state a claim upon which relief can be granted.

2. Defendant admits the allegations of Plaintiff's Complaint in paragraphs 1 and 2.

3. Defendant denies upon information and belief the remaining allegations in Plaintiff's Complaint.

WHEREFORE, Defendant requests that Plaintiff's claims be denied in their entirety and that Defendant receive all other such relief as appropriate and proper in this court.

_____
[SIGNATURE]

_____
Notary Seal

THE DISCOVERY STAGE

The longest part of a civil lawsuit is the time between filing the initial documents to begin the process and the time it takes the case to wind its way through the court system until trial. During that period, the rules may permit the parties to engage in investigating and discovering the "other side's" case. This stage is called "discovery." In this stage, the defendant attempts to learn the basis for the complaint and the identity of witnesses and experts who may testify at trial. The plaintiff learns more information about the defenses raised by the defendant. The purpose for discovery is to narrow the issues for trial, and to identify witnesses and documents to be utilized. There are specific rules for conducting discovery including the time within which documents can be filed and the content of the requests for information. Common discovery methods are by "motions" (formal requests for orders from the judge), "interrogatories" (written questions which the other side must answer), "depositions" (oral questions which the other side must answer under oath), or requests or subpoenas for documents.

Failure to respond to a discovery request can subject the party to serious sanctions, including the costs or fees of the other party in attempting to gain compliance or even a dismissal of the case. If a party has an objection to a discovery request as being unfair or unduly burdensome, that party can seek relief from the judge. The judge can also refuse to admit information gained through discovery at trial if it was obtained through an abuse of the discovery process.

DISCOVERY MOTIONS

During the discovery stage, several pretrial motions may be filed by either party. These motions may relate to the documents filed with the court, or may request the court to rule on some aspect of the case such as discovery disputes. One common motion filed in many personal injury cases is the "Motion for Physical or Mental Examination." This motion requests the court to require a party to undergo a physical or mental examination. If the judge determines that the physical or mental condition of the party is at issue, the judge can order the party to undergo the examination.

This motion is more commonly filed by the defendant as a way to limit a damage request. For example, if the plaintiff states that his or her right arm can no longer be used as a result of the injuries sustained during the crime, the defendant may want a physical examination of the plaintiff in the hope it will show that the plaintiff's arm had been damaged earlier, and thus the injuries were the result of the earlier injury, rather than due to the crime. Similarly, if the plaintiff states that he or she suffers debilitating mental anguish as a result of the crime, the defendant may ask for a mental examination in the hope of showing that the plaintiff suffered earlier mental problems that caused, or contributed significantly to, the mental anguish of the plaintiff.

INTERROGATORIES   Pursuant to the specific rules of the jurisdiction, each party is usually entitled to send the other a written list of questions requesting specific answers. These are called "interrogatories." They are an effective method of obtaining information. The party who answers the interrogatories answers them under oath so that he or she will be bound by the information provided.

DEPOSITIONS   A deposition is usually a series of oral questions, the answers to which are given under oath. They may be used to gather information or obtain evidence which can later be used against the party at trial. A deposition usually takes place at a law office or in a conference room, with a court reporter present. The questioning is very broad, and questions can be asked which go beyond the scope of what would be admissible at trial. A party or witness can be asked to bring documents or records to the deposition. The party seeking the deposition is responsible to pay for the court reporter's costs, which can be expensive.

Since the purpose of a deposition is to "lock-in" the testimony of a witness, preparation for an appearance at a deposition is very important. To prepare, become familiar with the nature of a deposition by viewing a deposition either in an actual trial on television, or on a videotape that might be available through the local public library or local bar association.

Look at any documents, like police reports, or your notes or diaries which will help you recall all of the relevant facts of the case, as well as what you may have said before. Read over any of the papers filed in court. Practice aloud your answers in front of a mirror or videotape yourself so that you can adjust your style of presentation. You have the right to prepare yourself for the deposition, and if you are asked at the deposition whether you "prepared" for it, you can truthfully answer "yes."

Dress comfortably, but neatly, for the deposition, which may last for several hours. You have the right to take breaks. At the deposition, the following rules should generally be followed:

- You will be sworn by the court reporter to tell the truth, and you must do so.

- Only bring to the deposition those documents that were specifically identified in the notice. (Do not bring any extra documents. It is not your job to help the other side.)

- You will be asked general identifying and background information, including name, address, family, and employment information. (If you were not required to provide address information in the complaint and if you fear for the safety of yourself or any member of your family, object to giving this information and request to have the judge rule on whether it must be provided.)

- Answer one question at a time. If the question is confusing or asks for several things, do not try to answer. Instead, ask for clarification of exactly what is being asked.

- Do not volunteer more information than is being asked. Remember that your deposition is for the benefit of the defendant, not you. Practice this. It is very difficult to get used to, because in ordinary conversation we tend to "fill in the blanks," but that isn't what you want to do at a deposition unless you are specifically asked a question that requires such an answer.

- Answer only with facts; not guesses. Everyone has limits to their knowledge. If you don't know the answer, say "I don't know." If you cannot remember something, say "I don't recall."

- Do not agree with the defendant's, or the defense attorney's, summary of what you said. Often the defense attorney will make a statement, or paraphrase what you have said, then ask you if that is correct. This is a strategy designed to put you at ease, so that the defense attorney can change your words slightly, which may be different from the meaning of your original answer. The attorney for the defendant is not your friend, no matter how "friendly" he or she seems.

- Be sure that any document shown to you is what you are told it is. Read the document before answering so that you are clear on what the document is.

- Do not let the questions make you so angry or upset that you answer with emotion instead of with fact. One of the purposes of a deposition is to see how you might respond to certain types of questions in the courtroom. Keep your composure. Do not get into arguments with the other side.

SUBPOENAS A subpoena may also be filed to require a party to produce documents or other items within that party's possession. These may then be copied, tested, or sampled by the other side for later use at trial.

SETTLING THE CASE

The long period before trial is also the time when settlement conferences may be held with a view towards resolving the case. The overwhelming majority of all types of lawsuits are settled prior to trial.

Many plaintiffs attempt to settle their case prior to filing the lawsuit which will save all parties time and expenses.

THE OFFER TO SETTLE

An offer to settle may be as simple as a direct letter to the defendant stating the facts and requesting compensation for injuries or damages. State the facts clearly and concisely and explain that you are prepared to sue if you do not receive satisfaction. Include a time limit by which you expect a response to the letter. Always keep copies of any correspondence you may initiate regarding the case. To prove that the defendant received the letter and had an opportunity to respond, send the letter by registered or certified mail-return receipt requested, or by another method by which the defendant will sign for receipt of the mailing.

An offer to settle may also be made after the suit is filed and the defendant is served with the initial complaint and summons. The defendant now understands that the threat of a lawsuit was serious and may be more ready to negotiate a settlement. If the defendant does make an offer to settle, make sure it is in writing and that any agreement is also in writing. This agreement becomes a binding document should the defendant later refuse to honor the terms of the agreement.

If the case is a simple one, the settlement and agreement can be completed at or before the first court date on the case. Then, if both parties agree, the judge will dismiss the case. In more complex cases, or cases in which a child is the victim, the judge will require a conference to review the terms of the agreement prior to dismissal.

THE SETTLEMENT CONFERENCE

In complex cases, the court may periodically require the parties to attend a settlement conference to see whether certain issues can be resolved prior to the trial date. At this conference, each party may prepare a pretrial memorandum listing its witnesses and issues to be resolved as well as the damages at issue. Many cases are settled after one or two conferences in which the judge, attorneys, and parties may be present.

ALTERNATIVE
DISPUTE
RESOLUTION

In the past few years, the courts have been unable to keep pace with the numbers of civil lawsuits of all kinds which have been filed. Alternative Dispute Resolution (ADR) has been adopted by some jurisdictions as a method of clearing the backlog of cases which are good prospects for settlement. There are two types of ADRs used in courts, but generally the parties either voluntarily or by court rule take their case to a neutral third party (usually an attorney or retired judge who has training in ADR) who hears the facts and arguments and makes a decision. The parties may agree in advance whether the decision is "binding" or not. For example, the cases in the TV show "People's Court" were an example of binding alternative dispute resolution.

THE SETTLEMENT
AGREEMENT

There is no set form for a settlement agreement, but most follow the topics listed in the complaint. Because it is a private action, the parties are free to agree to almost anything—as long as it is legal. A crime victim should be aware of certain pitfalls in settling the case against the offender. For example, if your criminal case is pending, you should not agree to cooperate in dropping the charges against the defendant. As a witness in the criminal case, you could be charged with filing a false police report or perjury if you change your testimony. Instead, the prosecutor should be notified about the civil case and the offer to settle. The prosecutor has the power to dismiss the case against the defendant or otherwise take into consideration that the defendant has paid the victim damages for the injury caused by the crime.

Another issue that frequently arises in negotiating a settlement is the defendant's desire to keep the terms of the settlement confidential. The defendant might be an insurance company that fears publicity, or it might be the offender who fears loss of reputation in the community. While the plaintiff may choose to agree to the demand for confidentiality, the plaintiff does not have to include such a provision into the agreement. If a confidentiality clause is included, either party may be liable for failure to comply with its terms.

PRESENTING THE CASE

Once the pre-trial stage ends, the case is set for trial, and final preparations are made to present the necessary evidence. If the case is not settled it will go to trial. The trial may be by judge or by jury, depending on the jurisdiction, the rules applicable to a given case, and whether either party has requested a jury trial. If the case is eligible to be heard by a jury, one must be requested in advance and certain fees paid. Generally, the trial will be before a judge alone, unless either party requests a jury. The role of the jury is to be the "factfinder." In a case with a jury, the judge's job is to explain to the jury how to apply the law to the facts. If no jury is requested or the case is not eligible to be tried by a jury, then the judge becomes both the "fact" and "law" finder.

THE OPENING
STATEMENT

The plaintiff begins the presentation of the case by making an opening statement. The plaintiff begins since he or she initiated the case and has the burden of proving that the defendant is liable. The defense may also make an opening statement, which may be immediately after the plaintiff's opening statement, or after the plaintiff has presented all of his or her evidence. The purpose of the opening statements are to outline the case for the judge or jury, so that they will understand each party's theory about what happened, how it happened, and what each party is asking. The opening statement is usually well-organized and fairly short, and simply provides each party's overview of the case.

Most plaintiffs' opening statements will include information about the nature of the case, the crime committed, what happened to the victim, the police investigation and arrest (if any) of the criminal, the medical injuries to the victim, why the defendant is responsible for what happened to the victim, and a request to compensate the victim and punish the defendant for the damages suffered.

If the defendant was not convicted in the criminal case, or is a third party (e.g., a landlord), the defendant's opening statement may counter that the crime was not his or her fault. The defendant may try to place

131

the blame on the victim for what happened, or may suggest that the victim was not injured to the extent suggested by the plaintiff. The defendant will ask that a verdict be returned in the defendant's favor (i.e., that the plaintiff not be awarded any money).

PROVING THE CASE

The plaintiff next presents evidence through witnesses' testimony and the production of exhibits (documents and other physical items). The defense has a right to cross-examine any of the plaintiff's witnesses in an attempt to clarify what they have said, add to what they have said, and impeach their credibility, thereby reducing the impact of their testimony in the case. Cross-examination can also be used to show any bias, interest, or motive of the witness.

The particular witnesses to be called in the case depend on the facts to be proven. Some of the same witnesses who testified in the criminal trial may be needed in the civil trial. In the absence of a conviction, or if proof of the crime is required, the police officers responsible for responding to and investigating your case will be called to testify. The medical personnel who provided you with treatment will testify as to the injuries you suffered after the crime, and any long-term or permanent injuries you suffered. Therapists or counselors may provide testimony on your psychological damages.

If proof of a third party's negligence is necessary, then those witnesses will be called to testify. For example, if a landlord failed to change or repair a broken lock, it might be necessary to call as witnesses other tenants who could testify as to their repeated requests for repairs.

If a conviction was obtained in the criminal case, a certified copy of that judgment can be obtained from the court clerk and used in the civil case as proof that the defendant committed the criminal act. In that case, the proof in the civil case will be primarily concerned with damages.

THE DEFENDANT'S CASE

After the plaintiff completes her or his case, the defendant is entitled to introduce evidence through the same methods. Similarly, the plaintiff is entitled to cross-examine the defendant's witnesses.

CLOSING
ARGUMENTS

Once each side has completed its case, the parties summarize the facts and evidence introduced through closing arguments. The purpose of the closing argument is for each party to pull together all the bits and pieces of evidence offered, and explain why the case should be decided in its favor. The plaintiff will remind the jury (or judge if there is no jury) of the testimony of each witness, and the items of evidence, that helps to prove the elements of the plaintiff's case. For example, if a police officer testified as to what he or she found at the crime scene, the plaintiff will remind the jury of what the officer said. If the emergency room physician testified as to the injuries of the plaintiff as a result of the crime, then the jury will also be reminded of this.

The request for damages should be clearly identified in the closing argument. Each item of damage requested should be stated and each item of loss that has a dollar value should be listed. For example, if the victim has lost 10 days of work, then the exact amount of lost wages and benefits would be valued. Each item of injury should be identified with the amount of loss it has caused to the victim. For example, if the victim lost 30% of the movement in his or her arm as a result of being shot by the criminal, then the jury should be reminded that this is a permanent loss to the victim. Finally, the victim's pain and suffering will also be listed as an item of damage for consideration.

In closing argument, the defendant will point out the weaknesses in the plaintiff's case. The defendant will argue that the plaintiff has the burden to prove all the elements of the case, otherwise there should be no recovery. The defendant will try to remove the element of emotion from the discussion of damages. The defendant will often say that despite the damage claims, there is no responsibility and therefore there can be no consideration of the dollars. Also, the defendant will remind the jury that damages have to be based upon proof, not mere guesses. If there is a finding in favor of the plaintiff, the defendant may argue that, at most, the plaintiff is entitled to be reimbursed; not to make a profit off the case. The defendant may emphasize how the plaintiff has returned to school or work, and has resumed daily activities which show recovery.

Also, the defendant may try to argue that the plaintiff is partially responsible and therefore the award should be reduced.

THE VERDICT, JUDGMENT, AND POST-TRIAL DECISIONS

THE VERDICT

After both parties have completed their closing arguments, if it is a jury case, the judge instructs the jury on the law to be applied in its deliberation and the case goes to the jury for consideration. The jury will decide whether the plaintiff has proved the case by a "preponderance of the evidence." If there is not a jury, the judge will decide these matters.

THE AWARD OF DAMAGES

If the jury determines that the plaintiff has proved the elements of his or her case, it next decides what amount to award the plaintiff. In tort law, each individual is presumed to intend all the natural and probable consequences of his or her deliberate acts, but the resulting injuries need not be foreseeable. For example, if the victim has a heart attack during a sexual assault, the defendant is liable for all those damages although he or she may argue that such an occurrence could not be foreseen.

The amount of money to award is a question of fact for the jury (or judge if there is no jury). The plaintiff can request an amount, but the jury may award a greater or lesser amount. The jury may also reduce an award on the basis that the victim "contributed" to the injuries.

THE JUDGMENT

Once the judge or jury finds in favor of the plaintiff or defendant, the judge incorporates that decision into a finalized document called a "judgment." The judgment is a formal document which includes a caption, description of the parties, statement of facts proved, findings, and a disposition of each of the items of relief requested. The trial judge signs the judgment and includes an effective date. Unless a post-trial motion for a new decision is granted, the judgment is the final permanent decision of the trial judge.

APPEAL AND
OTHER POST-
TRIAL
MANEUVERS

Any party may file "post-trial" motions seeking to change the decision in the case. One example of such a motion is called a "motion for judgment notwithstanding the verdict" in which the defense asks the judge to set aside the jury's verdict. If the verdict stands, the court enters the judgment, and either party has the right to an appeal.

ENFORCING THE JUDGMENT

Obtaining the judgment, or award of damages, may be the beginning of the final chapter rather than the end of the case. Collection of a judgment amount is the final goal, and may be challenging. Some criminals are "indigent" (i.e., they do not have any real assets from which to draw funds to pay the judgment amount). Other criminals are employed and do have some income. They may own a business or have other property assets which can be used to satisfy a judgment. Also, if the defendant inherits money or wins the lottery, those funds can be used to pay the victim's judgment. Finally, some criminals sue the government or the prison system for "civil rights" violations and recover monies. These can be used to satisfy a judgment in the victim's civil case.

"Son of Sam" laws may also provide funds for collection of a victim's judgment. These laws were passed after serial killer David Berkowitz sold the story of his murders for money.[15] Although the laws differ in each state, generally they require the victim to file a claim based on a civil judgment obtained within a certain period of time. When the criminal is convicted and receives profits, that money is then turned over to the state for distribution to the victim. In 1991, however, New York's Son of Sam law was declared unconstitutional because, among other things, it applied too broadly to include persons who had not been accused or convicted of crimes.[16] Check with your State Attorney General's Office to determine the status of the law, and your eligibility to access any such funds in your state.

If the defendant does have assets with which to satisfy the judgment but refuses to pay, the plaintiff can return to court to seek enforcement by attaching specific assets. For example, if the defendant is employed, a wage garnishment proceeding can be instituted in which a percentage of the defendant's income is withheld by the defendant's employer and paid directly to the plaintiff. If the defendant has real estate, the court can order confiscation through a "sale and levy" procedure whereby the property is sold at public auction or transferred to the plaintiff to satisfy the judgment.

A defendant may seek to avoid collection of a judgment by declaring bankruptcy. Generally, a judgment for intentional conduct is not dischargeable in bankruptcy, but a judgment based on negligence may be discharged.[17] The victim who obtains a judgment will be notified by the Bankruptcy Court if the defendant tries to obtain a discharge. File an "objection" with the Bankruptcy Court to establish that the conduct is not dischargeable. A defendant may be able to gain some relief from the judgment by filing a type of bankruptcy in which he or she agrees to pay a percentage of the judgment under a plan approved by a bankruptcy court.[18]   In this case, be sure to participate in the creditor's hearing on approval of the defendant's proposed plan of payment to ensure your rights.

SELECTED ISSUES AND CASES 20

While victims of a variety of crimes are beginning to access the civil justice system, two categories of crime in particular are somewhat new entrants: sexual assault and domestic violence. Perhaps the intimate nature of the crime, societal stigma, or lack of awareness of remedies has kept these victims from coming forward to seek civil justice until recently. Whatever the reason, that situation is changing, and suits by victims in these two categories are on the increase. A similar increase is seen in the number of cases filed against third parties who permit or allow the conditions to occur which victimize their employees, tenants, passengers, and others. One excellent resource for assistance, referral, and information concerning civil cases is "The Carrington Victims' Litigation Project" which is a program of the National Victim Center. The Project includes a database of information and can refer victims to attorneys nationwide. See Appendix D for more information.

SEXUAL ASSAULT VICTIMS

A sexual assault or sexual abuse is both a crime and a tort. Research discloses that thousands of women, children, and men are sexually victimized every year in the United States. Despite increasing awareness of the scope and prevalence of these crimes, criminal convictions remain challenging and a number of sexual assault victims are turning to the civil courts to seek justice.

Various theories are relied upon for recovery in civil suits based upon sexual assault. While many cases are filed against third parties due to the greater potential for settlement or collection of judgment, some cases are filed against the perpetrator

Most cases against the offender allege his or her intentional conduct as the basis for the suit. Theories include: assault (threats of physical harm), battery (physical injury), false imprisonment (detention of the victim), intentional infliction of emotional distress, rape, sexual abuse, and sexual assault. If the offender is a professional or an employer, there are several additional bases to support the suit, such as malpractice. If the offender is a parent, parental negligence or incest may be additional counts. Theories against third parties include: negligent hiring, retention, and supervision (against employers); and negligence in operation and maintenance of the premises (against hotels, daycare centers, etc.). Most cases allege several theories and seek recovery on as many bases as the facts will support.

The following representative cases are illustrative:

- School District held liable for failure to protect student from sexual abuse by physical education teacher. *Leija v. Canutillo Independent School District*, WL 355345 (Texas, 1995). Award: $1.4 million.

- Landlord liable for rape of tenant for failure to provide adequate security and for misrepresenting security. *Veazey v. Elmwood Plantation Assoc., Ltd.*, 646 So.2d 866 (Louisiana, 1994). Award: $180,000.

- Gynecologist liable for assault and battery, and medical malpractice for stimulating plaintiff's genital area as a "diagnostic procedure." (Michigan, 1985.) Settlement: $250,000.

SUITS BY ADULTS
FOR CHILDHOOD
SEXUAL ABUSE

One category of sexual assault victims who have increasingly turned to civil courts for recovery is adults who were childhood victims of sexual assault. To understand the nature of the procedural obstacles facing such victims in filing and maintaining civil suits, it is necessary to briefly discuss the nature of childhood sexual abuse and the injuries suffered by its victims.

Those who sexually offend against children are most likely to be someone who has gained the trust of the victim and is close to the victim. The most commonly reported cases are intra-familial, with fathers, stepfathers, and father-figures the most common offenders. These offenders successfully silence their victims through threats or bribery.

Abuse may begin when the child is very young, or at a vulnerable emotional time in the child's life. It may start with fondling, gradually increasing over time to other physical contact and sexual intercourse. Physical violence is not commonly employed since the overwhelming authority of the offender is usually sufficient to gain the child's compliance. The sexual abuse may be repeated in secrecy for years. The child keeps the secret fearing the consequences of disclosure.

The specific psychological impact of the abuse will vary from case to case, depending on the age of the victim when the abuse began, the length and frequency of occurrence, the type of acts involved, and the level of violence involved. Initially, the child may experience sleeping and eating disturbances, phobias, guilt, shame, anger, and heightened sexual interest. The most commonly reported long-term effects included depression, self-mutilation and suicidal behavior, eating and sleeping disturbances, drug or alcohol abuse, sexual dysfunction, inability to form intimate relationships, tendencies towards promiscuity and prostitution, and a vulnerability to revictimization.

As adults, childhood sexual abuse victims have also been found to meet the criteria for Post-Traumatic Stress Disorder (PTSD). PTSD is a clinically diagnosed mental disorder in which the victim avoids situations that stimulate recall of traumatic events or experiences. PTSD may not be identified, discovered, or treated until many years after the incidents of abuse.

The adult abused as a child may develop PTSD as a way of coping with the resulting trauma by psychologically repressing unacceptable experiences until a later time in life when she or he can cope with them. In certain severe cases, the victim may also develop a multiple personality disorder to block memory of traumatic experiences.

One way in which the trauma can be avoided is by avoiding situations that remind the victim of the abuse and that trigger the emotional or psychological trauma. This might be a factor in preventing victims from taking civil action against offenders.

Perhaps the biggest obstacle for adults who were victims of childhood sexual abuse is the problem posed by statutes of limitation, which set fixed periods of time in which legal rights may be acted upon. Ordinarily, the statute of limitation begins to run when the "cause of action" (i.e., the incident constituting the abuse) occurs. Thus, when the act of sexual abuse takes place, the tort arises. Generally, statute of limitation periods do not begin to run until a child reaches the age of majority.

Various reasons are given for establishing statutes of limitation, including judicial economy, lack of evidence over the passage of time, and the notion that a defendant should be protected from "stale" claims by a plaintiff who has been afforded a reasonable length of time to file and seek redress through the courts. When a statute of limitation has run, it is a complete defense to a suit.

The unfairness of applying a strict time for all cases led courts to apply what has been called "the discovery rule." This rule permits the date marking the start of the limitation period to be when the plaintiff "knew or should have known" that the injury occurred. The United States Supreme Court first upheld the rule in a case by a worker against his employer involving the inhalation of silicone dust at work causing silicosis, a latent disease which does not manifest itself for several years.[19]

The previous rule of law would have required the employee to file his lawsuit within two years of inhaling the dust, which was impossible because the employee had no way of knowing about the disease at that time. The Supreme Court determined that the lawsuit could be filed within two years after the employee found out (or should have found out) that he had the disease. Later cases included other toxic torts producing latent diseases, and medical malpractice cases (where the patient has no way of finding out about the malpractice until years after the act of malpractice is committed).

In the 1980s, adults who were sexually abused as children attempted to utilize this delayed discovery rule exception. Courts had extended the delayed discovery rule to cases involving fraudulent concealment of wrongdoing, but refused to apply it to the 1986 case of an adult in a federal civil suit in New York who sued her father for childhood sexual abuse.[20] The court reasoned that "the defendant did not actively conceal these wrongs through fraud, deception, or misrepresentation until the plaintiff had reached her majority."[21] Instead the court strictly applied the statute of limitation, thus denying the victim the opportunity to maintain her suit.

During that same year, the Washington Supreme Court decided another childhood sexual abuse case which was filed more than five years after the expiration of the Washington statute of limitation.[22] The victim contended that she had blocked out the memory of the abuse by her father until she entered therapy one year prior to filing her complaint. The court ruled against the plaintiff, because the plaintiff failed to show facts which could be proven, given the passage of time.[23]

Courts soon began to divide cases into what became known as "Type I" and "Type II" cases. In a Type I case, the plaintiff typically alleged that he or she knew about the sexual abuse at or before the age of majority, but was unaware that other physical or psychological problems were caused by the abuse. A Type II plaintiff, however, argued that due to the trauma of the experience, he or she has repressed the memory of the abuse until shortly before filing suit. Courts have been more sympathetic to the Type II case.

Courts began to adopt contrary approaches in these cases. In 1988, Montana held that the delayed discovery rule would not be applied in Type I cases.[24] Several cases were filed in California and the results also excluded Type I cases.[25] But a few states, like Wisconsin, ruled that the victim who did not repress her memory of the abuse, but instead was unable to determine the extent of her damages could maintain a lawsuit against her father.[26] Because of the refusal of most courts to extend the delayed discovery rule to Type I cases of childhood sexual abuse, victim advocates began to look to legislatures for change.

Beginning in the late 1980s, states began to adopt legislation extending the time within which an adult who was a victim of childhood sexual abuse could file a suit. Alaska, California, Colorado, Connecticut, Illinois, Iowa, Maine, Minnesota, Missouri, Montana, Nevada, South Dakota, Utah, Vermont, Virginia, and Washington have all adopted extensions for adults who were victims of childhood sexual abuse.[27] Most states have codified versions of the delayed discovery rule; some simply extending the time within which the suit must be filed.

The following representative case is illustrative:

- Adult daughter sexually abused as child by father sued at age 24 for assault and battery. *Hoult v. Hoult*, 57 F.3d 1 (1st Cir. 1995). Award: $500,000.

DOMESTIC VIOLENCE VICTIMS

Domestic violence is one of the most serious and pervasive crime issues facing the United States today. Women are the most often reported victims of domestic violence. The American Medical Association estimates that nearly four million women are victims of severe assaults by boyfriends and husbands every year in the United States.[28] Other victims include husbands, children, the elderly and other family members, and other persons involved in an intimate relationship. Domestic violence accounts for 16% of murders in large urban counties.[29] Children who witness or experience domestic violence are severely impacted. More than 85% of federal offenders jailed for violent crimes "witnessed or suffered domestic abuse as children."[30]

SUITS AGAINST THE ABUSER

Civil suits may be filed against the abuser. Most cases against the offender allege his or her intentional conduct as the basis for the suit. Theories include: verbal assault, sexual and physical battery, false imprisonment, intentional infliction of emotional distress, parental abduction, intentional interference with child custody, rape, sexual abuse, sexual assault, and wrongful death. Due to the relationship between the parties, however, many victims do not sue their offender.

SUITS AGAINST THIRD PARTIES

Police officers and municipalities are commonly seen as defendants in these type of suits. While ordinarily, municipalities are immune from liability for injuries negligently caused by police officers while performing their official duties, there is an exception where a "special duty" exists. The basis of the immunity is that the duty of the municipality is generally owed to the public at-large and not specifically to any individual. In a particularly egregious case, the State of Georgia was held immune from federal liability where a father beat his son on several occasions and social workers failed to protect the child. Eventually, the child was severely injured, suffering permanent brain damage.[31] In other cases, where the police failed to promptly respond to a "911" call, thereby allowing the criminal to injure the victim, the suit against the police was dismissed.[32]

However, if there is a special relationship between the victim and police, then there is an exception. In the case of domestic violence laws, various courts have held that such a special duty does exist.[33] Recently, the Illinois Supreme Court upheld the right of a victim to sue the County and County Sheriff for failing to prevent her abduction by her husband.[34] In that case, the plaintiff wife had obtained an Order of Protection against her husband for physically and mentally abusing her and the children during the marriage. Less than one month later, the husband began threatening the plaintiff at work. He threatened, among other things, to kill himself in front of the plaintiff and children unless

143

she came to him. The plaintiff telephoned police for assistance, stating that her husband was armed with a gun and had the child. The Sheriff of the local county travelled to where the husband was present, observed the residence, then drove off without taking any other action. The plaintiff contacted police again, but was told to contact her attorney. Within a few minutes the husband arrived at the plaintiff's work and forced the plaintiff to drive away with him at gunpoint. As police attempted to stop the vehicle, the plaintiff jumped out and the husband shot himself.[35]

In a New York case, an Order of Protection was obtained by a wife against her husband after numerous threats and assaults.[36] The husband continued to threaten the wife in violation of the Order of Protection, but was not arrested. During a visit with the children, the husband mutilated their six-year old child. Although the Order of Protection was granted to the wife, the court held that the children were also entitled to be protected.

The following representative cases are also illustrative:

- Domestic violence abuser who shot and killed victim liable for wrongful death. *Armstrong v. Randle*, 881 S.W.2d 53 (Texas 1994). Award: $491,700 compensatory damages and $5 million punitive damages.

- City liable for failure of police to enforce order of protection resulting in serious injuries to minor child during visitation with father. *Sorichetti v. City of New York*, 482 N.E.2d 70 (New York 1985). Award: $2,040,000.

CASES AGAINST THIRD PARTIES

PLANES, TRAINS, AND OTHER COMMERCIAL CARRIERS

It is impossible to list all the potential third parties who may have contributed, or been partly responsible for, the injuries sustained by the victim, but some examples will help clarify the types of third parties commonly seen in victim's litigation:

A common carrier, such as a bus, train, taxi, ship, or plane, owes a high degree of care to its passengers to provide safe passage and can be held liable for failing to fulfill that duty. For example, where a railroad has knowledge that a certain train runs through a "high crime" area and yet fails to adequately supervise the area or provide security for the passengers, it can be held liable.

Cases:

- Cruise line liable for attack on woman passenger in a stateroom. *Holland America Cruises, Inc. v. Underwood*, 470 So.2d 19 (Florida 1985). Award: $130,000.

- Rider on an "El" train sued Chicago Transit Authority (CTA) for failure to lock the vacant compartments, resulting in a sexual assault. (Illinois 1982.) Award: $200,000.

- Long Island Railroad held liable for sexual assault on a railroad employee in the parking lot of one of its stations, for failure to provide adequate lighting. (New York 1973.) (Award reduced 10% due to contributory negligence of victim.) Award: $1.75 million.

- Greyhound Bus Company held liable for dropping 14-year-old plaintiff off at a dangerous location without security after she missed her stop. Plaintiff accepted a ride from a motorist who sexually assaulted her. (Federal Court, Oregon 1980.) Settled: $235,000.

- Greyhound Bus Company held liable for failure to maintain security at a depot where plaintiff was sexually assaulted in the women's restroom. *Wesley v. Greyhound Lines, Inc.*, 268 S.E.2d 855 (North Carolina 1980). Award: $150,000.

- Metropolitan Atlanta Transit Authority held liable for rape of woman at night in parking lot. (Georgia 1988.) Award: $250,000.

EMPLOYER An employer has a duty to provide a reasonably safe work environment for its employees. Furthermore, certain employers have a duty to check the background of their employees and to properly supervise those employees in their tasks. The employer also has a duty to take reasonable steps when it has notice of complaints regarding employee conduct, and the victim may show that the employer was negligent for retaining the employee. If the conduct occurs outside of the employee's "scope of employment," then the victim must show that the crime was foreseeable or incidental to the employment.

Cases:

- Negligent retention of taxicab driver who raped passenger. *Fort Worth Cab & Baggage Co, Inc. v. Salinas*, 735 S.W.2d 303 (Texas 1987). Award: $4.4 million.

- Shooting of laundromat customer by employee over argument about missing shirts. *Weinberg v. Johnson*, 518 A.2d 985 (Wash. D.C. 1986). Award: $2,000,000.

- Bar patron beaten by bouncer employed by bar. *Country Roads, Inc. v. Witt*, 737 S.W.2d 362 (Texas 1987). Award: $15,500 compensatory and $50,000 punitive damages.

- Manager approved security guards' beating of customer. *Cerminara v. California Hotel and Casino*, 760 P.2d 108 (Nevada 1988). Award: $100,000 punitive damages.

- Drunk driver employee, on way home from employment dinner, killed victim. *Carroll Air Systems, Inc. v. Greenbaum*, 629 So.2d 914 (Florida 1993). Award: $800,000.

- Failure to conduct proper background investigation of employee who raped victim-customer in her home. *Smith v. Orkin Exterminating Co., Inc.*, 540 So.2d 363 (Louisiana 1989). Award: $125,000.

HOTEL; MOTEL; BUILDING OWNER; OR LANDLORD

Hotels, motels, landlords, other innkeepers such as vacation resorts, hotel chains, and individual "bed and breakfast" lodges, or any other business enterprise which provides lodging or is responsible for property, must use reasonable care to protect its customers or tenants from assault.

Where a motel or hotel operator fails to provide adequate security, control the room keys properly, or provide adequate door locks, liability will attach.

A landlord is responsible to keep the common areas—stairs, hallway, roof, lobby, basement—over which he or she has control in a reasonably safe condition, and will be held liable for negligent maintenance of these areas. Landlords have been held liable for failing to repair defective locks on common area doors, failing to maintain security lighting, and storage of a ladder outside the victim's apartment which had been used previously in a burglary. Liability has also been imposed where a landlord purports to provide a security service but does so negligently. For example, the owner of a motel, or a landlord, who fails to reasonably take adequate steps to protect persons on the property (such as by installing adequate locks or security doors, or hiring security guards) may be held responsible for contributing to the environment which led to the crime.

Cases:

- Hotel liable for rape of victim on premises. *Splawn v. Lextaj Corp.*, 603 N.Y.S.2d 41 (New York 1993). Award: $2. million.

- Female guest of hotel raped due to negligent security. *Garzilli, et.al. v. Howard Johnson's Motor Lodges, Inc.*, 419 F. Supp. 1210 (New York 1976). Settled: $1.5 million; husband settled for $25,000 for loss of companionship.

- Motel owner held liable for robbery and assault when clerk gave victim's room key to stranger. *Kraaz v. LaQuinta Motor Inns, Inc.*, 410 So.2d 1048 (Louisiana 1982). Award: $73,000.

- Landlord held responsible where victim physician was shot and seriously injured. *Sinai v. Polinger Co.*, 498 A.2d 520 (Washington, D.C. 1985). Award: $1.5 million.

- Assailant entered plaintiff's apartment through open window. Plaintiff was 96 years old at time of attack and lived in a complex for the elderly. Landlord failed to limit access to the roof. (California 1985.) Verdict: $65,000 less 10% victim's contributory negligence for leaving her window open! Final award: $58,500.

SHOPPING CENTER; RESTAURANT

The shopping center is analogous to a landlord in terms of liability. Each store owner/tenant is charged with the duty to maintain the individual premises, while the center usually maintains the common areas. In the case where a center undertakes the responsibility of contracting for services to individual stores, it will be liable for negligence in maintaining such service. The usual bases for liability of a shopping center are inadequate security, lighting, maintenance, and negligent supervision of employees.

Cases:

- Customer injured when knocked to the ground by shoplifter fleeing store. *Allied Stores of Texas, Inc. v. McClure*, 622 S.W.2d 618 (Texas 1981). Award: $35,000.

- Store held liable for broken hip of employee during attack by purse snatcher. *General Syndicators of America v. Green*, 522 So.2d 1081 (Florida 1988). Award: $54,000 to employee, and $5,000 to employee's spouse for loss of consortium.

- Shopping center owner held liable for failure to provide adequate security where plaintiff store employee was abducted while leaving work. (Delaware 1985.) Award: $530,000 compensatory and $250,000 punitive damages.

SCHOOL; DAY CARE; HOSPITAL

The duty of a hospital, or a school, day care center, or other education institution is to provide a reasonably safe environment for its staff and students. Negligent supervision of teachers or premises, retention of employees after notice of complaints, failure to investigate the background of employees, and failure to maintain adequate security will result in liability.

Cases:

- County social service agency held liable for failure to properly supervise day care center. Preschool teacher sexually assaulted 7 year-old boy enrolled at day care. (Nevada 1986.) Award: $200,000 (One of 25 children assaulted by same teacher).

- Teachers, principal, and school held liable for sexual assault of 10 year-old boy. (California 1985.) Award: $680,000 to victim; $100,000 to mother.

- Day care center held liable for sexual assault of 5 year-old girl by sons of center owner. (California 1986.) Award: $453,000.

- University held liable for assault on woman while waiting in the parking lot. (Washington, D.C., 1986.) Settled: $150,000.

- Hospital held liable for failure to protect patient in restraint from assault by another patient. *Freeman v. St. Clare's Hospital & Health Center*, 156 A.D.2d 300 (New York, 1989). Award: $125,000.

POLICE AND GOVERNMENT

Generally, police officers or other public officials of the government do not owe a special duty to any one individual. But under certain circumstances, the police have been held to have a "special relationship" with the victim and therefore were liable for failing to protect or prevent the criminal acts. Cases may be filed in state court, but also in Federal Court if the public officials acted under "color of law" (i.e., using the authority of their position) during a civil rights violation.

Cases:

- Municipality held liable where victim called police, but dispatcher sent police to wrong address and no follow-up conducted, resulting in victim being stabbed to death by intruder. *DeLong v. Erie County*, 457 N.E.2d 717 (New York 1982). Award: $800,000.

- Municipality liable where victims were killed by suspect who was under surveillance by police, where police withdrew protection

149

without notice to the victims. *Zibbon v. Town of Cheektowaga,* Chicago Tribune, Dec. 3, 1978, Sec. 3, p. 30. Award: $100,000.

• Federal civil rights violated when police arrested drunk driver, impounded vehicle, and left female passenger in a high crime area where she accepted a ride from a stranger who raped her. *Wood v. Ostrander,* 879 F.2d 583 (9th Cir. 1989).

THE ROLE OF LAWYERS 21

The role of lawyers in civil suits is completely different than in the criminal justice system. Unlike the criminal case, there is no lawyer involvement in a civil case unless a party hires a lawyer. If you want a lawyer, you will have to hire one or find one who will take the case without charge. Remember that the defendant does not have a right to have a lawyer appointed either.

Recognize that the law is a business as well as a profession. Your decision to hire an attorney may be based on the complexity of your case. Attorneys also make decisions on whether to accept a case based on a number of factors. For example, an attorney is likely to consider the potential for collection from the defendant prior to committing resources towards the case.

In evaluating a case, an attorney will examine:

- Cost

- Time and Effort

- Potential for Collection

LAWYERS AND CONFIDENTIALITY

To encourage people to speak freely to their lawyers, the law provides confidentiality protection for clients. This is called the "attorney-client privilege." The privilege prevents a lawyer from disclosing your information under most circumstances, so be honest in disclosing all the facts, even those facts about the crime or yourself which are embarrassing or humiliating. The lawyer needs this information to properly evaluate the case.

FINDING A LAWYER

The search for a lawyer can take some time and no small amount of perseverance. Just as there are specialities in other professions, it is becoming rarer today to find a lawyer that has a general practice. Many lawyers limit their practice to certain types of cases, such as family law, estate planning, corporate law, etc. The lawyer you choose should have some experience in similar cases, and it would be ideal if he or she had filed a civil suit on behalf of a crime victim prior to your case.

RECOMMENDATIONS FROM FRIENDS

Many times a lawyer is chosen through the help of recommendations by family or friends. These recommendations can be helpful because the good experience of your family member or friend may provide reliable information on the quality of service provided by the lawyer.

REFERRAL SERVICES

If you do not personally know a lawyer and do not have a recommendation from a trusted friend or family member, you can look to other sources. In most cities there is a local "bar association" which is an organization to which many local attorneys will belong. The bar association can help make lawyer referrals, either formally or informally. Sometimes, a recent judgment or settlement of a personal injury lawsuit is publicized and the plaintiff's lawyer's name is listed. Recently, some lawyers have begun to advertise on television or radio. Your victim/witness coordinator or victim advocate from your criminal case may also be able to provide you with resources.

LAW SCHOOL PROGRAMS

One often overlooked resource is a clinic program in a law school. Some law schools maintain programs which take cases of public interest in particular areas. Be sure to check with the law schools in your state to see whether such programs exist and whether your case would qualify. If the clinic accepts your case, you may not be required to pay or your fee will be substantially reduced.

ATTORNEY REGISTRATION

Every state maintains a registration of lawyers who practice law within that state. To find the phone number and address of any lawyer within your state, contact the bar association or other attorney registration office in your state. Look in the phone book, ask your prosecutor (who will also be registered), or contact your state Attorney General's Office for assistance. To find your local bar association, simply look in the yellow pages for the listing under "lawyer referrals."

INITIAL CONTACT

The selection of a lawyer usually begins with a phone call. In this first contact with the lawyer, be sure to obtain some preliminary information. Does this lawyer have experience in your type of case? Will you be charged for the first visit? How long will you meet for the first visit? How much does this lawyer usually charge for services? Compare the answers given by the lawyers you speak to, then decide which one to meet with for an initial consultation about your case.

FIRST INTERVIEW

The initial interview with a lawyer is very important. Remember that you have not agreed to anything other than the terms of the initial visit. Do not be intimidated by the thought of meeting with the lawyer. You are under no obligation to sign or agree to anything at this time, and you can take any written documents home to think about before you sign. Follow your instincts and trust your evaluation of the person before you. Do you like this lawyer? Do you feel that he or she is listening to you and your story? Are you treated with respect during the visit by the office staff? Your "gut" will tell you much about whether you wish to proceed further with this lawyer.

In telling the lawyer about your case, be as clear and concise as possible. You might write out certain points to be sure you cover the important issues so that the lawyer can properly evaluate your case. Be sure to bring any relevant documents (police reports, court records from the criminal case, etc.) which will help the lawyer to understand your facts.

Discuss what the attorney believes the projected costs to be and how you will be billed for those costs. For example, if deposition transcripts and expert witnesses are to be retained, are those costs passed on to you or will those persons wait until the end of the case?

FEE AGREEMENTS

It is essential that you understand how the lawyer charges fees and costs. Most attorneys are expensive; charging more than $100 per hour, so sometimes the primary consideration in hiring a lawyer is your ability to pay. In recognition of this limitation, some attorneys who believe the case is meritorious will accept a "contingent fee" arrangement, in which they agree to wait until the end of the case to obtain their fee. The usual agreement states that if there is a judgment, the attorney is entitled to a percentage of the judgment as the fee (usually 1/3 to 40%), but if there is no award of damages, no fee will be due. The plaintiff is still responsible for "costs" (e.g., filing fees, photocopying, telephone charges, postage, transcript, and reporter fees).

Other attorneys charge by the hour up to a certain amount, and require a substantial initial payment from the victim. These attorneys feel that the victim's investment is essential and is a fair balance for the lawyer's consideration, time, and effort. Fees remaining up to a ceiling amount (such as 33% of the recovery) will be due only if there is a judgment or settlement award.

Make sure that you secure your fee agreement in writing so that there will be no confusion as to what is due and when. The agreement should clearly state whether an initial payment is due (sometimes called a "retainer") and how it should be paid; and whether there is an hourly fee rate charged or a "contingent" fee arrangement. The types of costs and methods by which those costs will be paid should be identified in the agreement.

If a retainer is to be paid, be sure you and your lawyer agree what minimal services are to be provided. For example, for a retainer of $500 or more, the lawyer should at least prepare and file a complaint and have it served on the defendant (or defendants). What you want to avoid is a situation where you pay your lawyer a retainer, he or she writes a letter and makes a few phone calls to the defendant, then tells you the retainer is used up and more money is required to continue.

WORKING WITH THE LAWYER

Once you have made a decision to hire the lawyer, and the lawyer agrees to take the case, be sure to let the lawyer know what kind of "client" you are. How involved do you want to be in the case? Do you want to be informed of each step in the case? Would you like copies of each document the lawyer files or receives in your case? Realize that you may be expected to pay for copies if there are costs involved. Alternatively, you may ask your lawyer to make the file available to you on a regular basis to view at his or her office to keep current with developments in your case.

Your lawyer should be able to take you through the case step-by-step to explain the procedures and anticipated timeline in your case. Ask the lawyer how often you can expect him or her to notify you about your case. If you know the general timeline of your case, it will help you understand how often to expect contact from the lawyer. For example, once your initial documents are filed, it may be at least 30 days (or longer) before the defendant files any documents in the case. Set up a method of contact that is convenient for you and reasonable for your lawyer. Many problems can be resolved by clear communications between the plaintiff and the lawyer.

APPENDIX A
SAMPLE FORMS

Form A. Request Letter to Police

Note: Write this letter to the officer in charge of your case. If you do not know which officer to address your request to, then send it to the police department in care of the police chief.

[Your Name]
[Your Street Address]
[Your City, State, Zip Code]

[Date]

Re: *[identify your case, include police report number if you have one, or date of crime if not]*

Dear   *[Name or individual if known, if not address to "Investigator," "Detective," "Chief," etc.]*

I was the victim of a *[type of crime]* on *[date]*. Under the victim's rights law of this state, I am hereby requesting that you keep me informed as to the status of the investigation. Please provide me with the name and contact number for the officer assigned to my case.

Please contact me to confirm that you have received this letter. *[Give contact information here: e.g., "I can be contacted in the daytime at 555-9999 or 123 South Street, Apt. 202"]*. I look forward to hearing from you.

Thank you,

[Your signature]
[Your name typed or printed]

Form B. Request for information from prosecutor

Note: Write this letter to the prosecutor in charge of your case. If you do not know which prosecutor to address your request to, then send it to the office of the prosecutor (sometimes called district attorney or state's attorney or county attorney).

[Your Name]
[Your Street Address]
[Your City, State, Zip Code]

[Date]

Re: *[Identify your case, including police report number if you have one, or date of crime if not]*

Dear *[Name of prosecutor if known, or "Prosecuting Attorney"]*:

I was the victim of a *[type of crime]* on *[date]*. I hereby request a copy of the victim's rights laws of our state. I also request that you keep me informed as to the following: *[arrest, filing of charges, bail release of defendant, advance notice of hearings, and continuances, an opportunity to confer with you before you make a plea agreement]*. Finally, please provide the name of the attorney responsible for prosecuting my case and a contact number.

I look forward to prosecuting my case. Please contact me to confirm that you have received this letter. *[Give contact information here, e.g., "I can be contacted in the daytime at 555-9999 or 123 South Street, Apt. 202"]*. I look forward to hearing from you.

Thank you,

[Your signature]
[Your name typed or printed]

Form C. Request for Prisoner Information

Note: Once the offender is incarcerated, write this letter to the department of corrections or prisoner review/parole board/county sheriff/juvenile detention center or mental health facility. If you do not know which department to address your request to, then contact your prosecuting attorney for information.

[Your Name]
[Your Street Address]
[Your City, State, Zip Code]

[Date]

Re: *[Identify your case, including court docket number if you have one]*

Dear *["Warden," "Parole Board," "Review Board," etc.]*:

I was the victim of *[type of crime]*. The offender's name is *[name of prisoner]*. The date of conviction is *[date]*. Under the crime victim's rights laws of this state, I request that you keep me informed as to status of the prisoner in advance if possible, including: escape and recapture, release for work or furlough purposes, community release or transfer to a mental health facility, and final release date. Finally, please provide the date, time and location of any parole, pardon or commutation procedures which may be scheduled in this case. In addition, I would like to know the name and contact number of the probation or parole officer assigned to the case.

Please contact me to confirm that you have received this letter. *[give contact information here, eg., I can be contacted in the daytime at 555-9999 or 123 South Street, Apt. 202"]*. I look forward to hearing from you.

Thank you,

[Your signature]
[Your name typed or printed]

Form D. Victim Impact Statement

Note: This statement is to be considered prior to sentencing the offender. Therefore it should be completed as soon as possible after the charges have been filed. Check with your prosecutor to see if they have a form for you to follow or use the one below.

Victim Impact Statement

CASE: State v. _____ [name of offender]
DOCKET/CASE NUMBER: _____
CRIME [list crimes here]:

_____
_____

Victim Information:

NAME _____ AGE_____PHONE_____
ADDRESS_____ CITY_____
STATE_____
WORK ADDRESS_____ CITY_____
STATE____

I WAS THE VICTIM OF: [describe crime]

_____
_____

Loss Suffered
[complete sections which apply to your case; attach documentation where possible]

I WAS PHYSICALLY INJURED: [include description of medical care or emergency treatment, hospitalization; list all doctors and hospitals; explain doctor's treatment, therapy, etc; Anticipated future physical impairment based on medical evaluation or doctor's statement]

_____
_____
_____
_____
_____

AMOUNT OF MEDICAL EXPENSES:

$_____ (TO DATE:_____)

$_____ (ANTICIPATED)

I WAS PSYCHOLOGICALLY INJURED: [include description of psychiatric or psychological care or treatment, hospitalization; explain doctor's treatment, counseling, therapy, etc; Anticipated future counseling, therapy, psychiatric care]

_____

_____

_____

_____

AMOUNT OF COUNSELING/THERAPY EXPENSES:

$_____ (TO DATE:_____)

$_____ (ANTICIPATED)

THIS CRIME AFFECTED ME PERSONALLY BY: [describe emotional injury, change in life-style, change in attitude, change in family/social relationships, hardships endured as a result of this crime] _____

_____

_____

_____

_____

_____

THIS CRIME AFFECTED MY FAMILY BY: [describe emotional injury, change in life-style, change in attitude, change in family/social relationships]

_____

_____

_____

_____

_____

I HAVE INCURRED EMPLOYMENT-RELATED LOSS: [include description of how this has affected your ability to earn a living, loss of job, wages, days, anticipated future loss]

_____

_____

_____

_____

I AM/AM NOT ELIGIBLE FOR WORKMEN'S COMPENSATION. IF COVERED, I HAVE/ HAVE NOT APPLIED.

    AMOUNT OF EMPLOYMENT EXPENSES:
    $_____ (TO DATE:_____)
    $_____ (ANTICIPATED)

I HAVE INCURRED PROPERTY-RELATED LOSS: [include description of property, damages or loss, cost to repair, replace loss]

_____
_____
_____
_____

IS PROPERTY IN CUSTODY OF POLICE? _____

    AMOUNT OF PROPERTY LOSS:
    $_____ (TO DATE:_____)
    $_____ (ANTICIPATED)

I HAVE INCURRED OTHER LOSS: [include description of other damages or loss]

_____
_____
_____
_____
_____

    AMOUNT OF LOSS:
    $_____ (TO DATE:_____)
    $_____ (ANTICIPATED)

BEING A VICTIM OF A CRIME: [include your feelings about the criminal justice process, and how you feel about your role in this case]

_____
_____
_____
_____
_____
_____

_____
_____
_____
_____
_____
_____

ALTHOUGH THE JUDGE WILL MAKE THE DECISION ON THE APPROPRI-
ATE SENTENCE I WOULD LIKE TO SEE THE OFFENDER BE SENTENCED
TO: [include any or all of the following - PROBATION, RESTITUTION, JAIL OR
PRISON, OTHER]
DESCRIBE ANY OTHER INFORMATION YOU WANT THE COURT TO CON-
SIDER.

To the best of my knowledge, the above information is true and correct. I understand that filing a claim for restitution does not affect my right to file a civil suit or
apply for Crime Victim's Compensation.

_____

Your Name   Date

Form E. Sample Civil Complaint
(Baby-sitter Abused Child)

IN THE NINTH CIRCUIT COURT, FOR JEFFERSON COUNTY
STATE OF COLUMBIA

C.D., by John Doe, as next friend and Guardian.))	
Plaintiff,)	
v.)	Case No. _____
)	
Susan Smith , Defendant.)	

COMPLAINT

COMES NOW, the minor plaintiff above named, by her Parent , John Doe, and files this Complaint against the defendant, for the following:

1. The plaintiff is C.D., a minor, and is the natural daughter of John Doe. Plaintiff resides at 123 Elm Street, Anytown, Columbia. The plaintiff was born on April 1, 1991.

2. The plaintiff brings this action by and through John Doe, her parent, who resides at 123 Elm Street, Anytown, Columbia.

3. The defendant is Susan Smith, and resides at 47259 Borden Road, Anytown, Columbia. The defendant was at all times relevant herein the baby-sitter of the plaintiff.

4. At all times herein mentioned, the defendant was charged with the supervision, care, custody, and control of the minor plaintiff in her capacity as baby-sitter.

5. On or about the end of July, 1996, the plaintiff's parents hired the defendant and delegated all of their duties as natural parents to the said "baby sitter" for those periods of time when the baby-sitter had care and control of the minor plaintiff.

6.   On August 14, 1996, while the minor plaintiff was in the sole custody and care of the defendant, the minor plaintiff was beaten about the face and body by defendant, sustaining severe, serious, and permanent injuries as more specifically hereinafter set forth.

7.   That the damages and injuries sustained by the minor plaintiff were caused and were the direct and proximate result of the intentional and negligent wrongful acts of the baby-sitter, specifically:

(a)   That the defendant did willfully and maliciously strike, beat, kick, and otherwise harm the plaintiff;

(b)   That the defendant was not competent to perform the duties of caring for the plaintiff and failed to exercise the requisite proper skill or experience;

8.   That by reason of the carelessness, recklessness, negligence, and intentional conduct of the defendant, the minor plaintiff sustained severe and serious injuries of a permanent nature, specifically:

(a)   Abrasions of the eyes, mouth, and ears;
(b)   Brain contusion;
(c)   Motor and visual problems.

9.   That as a result of said injuries, the plaintiff was required to receive medical care and treatment, x-rays, hospitalization, and other proper and necessary things in an effort to restore her health and will, by reason of said injuries, be required to undergo additional and similar medical care and treatment for the rest of her life.

10.   That as a result of said injuries and the consequences thereof, the plaintiff has suffered great physical pain and agony, inconvenience, and mental anguish; and will continue to suffer considerable pain and agony, inconvenience, and mental anguish in the future for the rest of her life.

WHEREFORE, plaintiff (C.D.), brings this action against the defendant to recover damages for a sum in excess of $ 250,000.00 Dollars.

_____

[SIGNATURE]

The State listings in this appendix are in alphabetical order, and give references for relevant victims' rights laws. The following information is given for each state:

THE LAW: This gives the official title of the set of books containing the state's statutes or code. It may also give other information that will help you locate particular sections of the law. Words in italics are the names of the publishers that are part of the title that appears on the volumes. Be sure to check for the latest updates of the statutes or code. These updates will either be found in a supplemental booklet inside the back cover of each volume, in a separate section of loose-leaf volumes, or in a separate supplemental book.

CRIME VICTIM COMPENSATION: This gives the citation to the particular statute or code section that deals with obtaining compensation from the state's crime victim compensation program. In addition to the statute or code, you may also want to see the book *Victims' Rights*, by William L. Ginsburg, which provides detailed information about applying for crime victim compensation from such programs.

VICTIMS' RIGHTS: This provides the citation to the particular statute of code section dealing with specific rights afforded to crime victims. It also gives a summary of those provisions.

STATUTES OF LIMITATION: This gives the citation to the particular statute or code sections relating to how much time a victim has in which to file a civil lawsuit against the offender or a third party, and gives a summary of these limitation periods.

Alabama

THE LAW: Code of Alabama

CRIME VICTIM COMPENSATION: §§15.23.1 to 15.23.23.

VICTIMS' RIGHTS: §§15-23-60 to 15-23-84 and Constitutional Amendment 557.
- Applies to felonies involving physical/personal injury, sex offenses, or family violence.
- Victim may designate a representative or court may appoint one for incapacitated victim; a parent may act as representative for child victim.
- Within 72 hours police must give the victim contact information, including name and phone number of prosecutor.
- Prosecutor must confer with victim prior to disposition of case.
- Victim has right to be present at trial, and may be seated at counsel table with prosecutor.
- Notice includes protection methods for intimidation; court must provide safe waiting area to minimize contact with defendant.
- Victim may present oral and written impact statement at sentencing and to parole board.
- Victim has right to notice of release, escape, or death of offender.

STATUTES OF LIMITATION:
Injury to person or sexual abuse discovery: §6-2-34.
Length of time: 6 years.

Alaska

THE LAW: Alaska Statutes

CRIME VICTIM COMPENSATION: §§18.67.010 to 18.67.180.

VICTIMS' RIGHTS: §§12.61.010 to 12.61.030; and Constitutional Amendment, Art. 1 Sec. 24, Art. II §24.
- Applies generally to all victims; additional rights for felonies and domestic violence.
- Victim impact statement can include opinion on restitution and recommendation of sentence.
- Restitution law (§12.55.045).

STATUTES OF LIMITATION:
Injury to person or sexual abuse discovery: §09.10.070.
Length of time: 2 years.
Sexual abuse discovery: §09.10.141(b)
Length of time: More than 3 years after the plaintiff reaches the age of majority if it is brought under the following:
Conditions: (1) if the claim asserts that the defendant committed one act of sexual abuse on the plaintiff, the plaintiff must commence the action with 3 years after the plaintiff discovered or through use of reasonable diligence should have discovered that the act caused the injury or condition; (2) if the claim asserts that the defendant committed more than one act of sexual abuse on the plaintiff, the plaintiff shall commence the action within 3 years after the plaintiff discovered or through use of reasonable diligence should have discovered the effect of the injury or condition attributable to the series of acts; a claim based on an assertion of more than one act of sexual abuse is not limited to plaintiff's first discovery of the relationship between any one of those acts and the injury or condition, but may be based on plaintiff's discovery of the effect of the series of acts.

Arizona

THE LAW: Arizona Revised Statutes

CRIME VICTIM COMPENSATION: §41-240-1.

VICTIMS' RIGHTS: §§13-4401 to 13-4415; and Constitutional Amendment, Art. II Sec. 2.1.
- Constitutional Amendment gives victim right to refuse interview, deposition, or other discovery request.
- Applies to felonies or misdemeanor involving physical injury, sex offenses, and juvenile cases.
- Victim may designate a representative; court may appoint one for incapacitated victim; parent may represent a child.
- Police must give the victim rights form, police report, contact numbers, and information on nearest crisis services.
- Within 7 days of filing charge, prosecutor must give victim notice of rights.
- Request notification of offender's release on bond, escape, and recapture.
- Right to be present at court proceedings; may request to confer with prosecutor.
- May present impact information and opinion on appropriate sentence at plea hearing; court will not accept plea unless prosecutor made efforts to consult with victim and victim had notice of hearing; restitution is mandatory.

STATUTES OF LIMITATION:
Injury to person or sexual abuse discovery: §12-541.
Length of time: 1 year.
Conditions: 2-years for assault and battery; 1-year for false imprisonment.

Arkansas

THE LAW: Arkansas Code of 1987 Annotated.

CRIME VICTIM COMPENSATION: §§16-90-701 to 16-90-718.

VICTIMS' RIGHTS: §16-21-106.
- Applies to all crimes and victims.
- Victim entitled to notice of scheduled hearings and continuances or changes of schedule.
- Prosecutors shall assist persons to obtain protection from intimidation.
- Notice of financial services, social services, and employer intercession where needed.
- Entitled to prompt return of property used as evidence.
- Victim has right to be present at trial and hearings (Evid. Rule 616).
- Court should, when possible, provide secure waiting area to minimize contact with defendant.
- Right to prepare and present a Victim Impact Statement (§16-97-103).

STATUTES OF LIMITATION
Injury to person or sexual abuse discovery: §16-56-104.
Length of time: 1 year.

California

THE LAW: *West's* Annotated California Codes. These books are divided into sets of volumes according to subject, such as "Government Code," "Probate Code," etc., so be sure you have the correct subject volume.

CRIME VICTIM COMPENSATION: Government Code §13959-74.

VICTIMS' RIGHTS: Penal Code §§679.02, 679.03; and Constitutional Amendment, Art. I Sec. 28.
- Applies to felonies, misdemeanors, and juvenile cases.
- Parents may represent minor child, and next of kin may represent a deceased victim.
- Consideration of bail must include, as a primary consideration, protection of public.
- Victim may be present on same basis as defendant (Penal Code §1102.6), and is entitled to a support person in court.
- Entitled to notice of scheduled hearings and charges, witness fees, civil claim information, and prompt return of property used as evidence.
- Prosecutor must notify victim of pretrial plea agreement before presentation to court.
- May request to make oral or written Victim Impact Statement at sentencing and parole consideration.
- Restitution is mandatory whether or not defendant receives probation (Government Code §13967); restitution order is enforceable as a civil judgment.
- Notice of release, escape, furlough, work release, or parole.

STATUTES OF LIMITATION:
Injury to person or sexual abuse discovery: Civil Procedure Code §340.
Length of time: 1 year
Sexual abuse discovery: Civil Procedure Code §340.1
Length of time: 3 years after the date the plaintiff discovers or reasonably should have discovered that psychological injury or illness occurring after the age of majority was caused by the sexual abuse, which ever occurs later.
Conditions: (1) Every plaintiff 26 years of age or older at the time the action is filed must file certificates of merit as specified in by law; (2) Certificates of merit must be executed by the attorney for the plaintiff and by a licensed mental health practitioner selected by the plaintiff; (3) A complaint filed pursuant to (1 above) may not name the defendant or defendants until the court has reviewed the certificates of merit filed and has found, in camera (i.e., in a private hearing), based solely on those certificates of merit, that there is reasonable and meritorious cause for the filing of the action. At that time, the complaint may be amended to name the defendant or defendants.

Colorado

THE LAW: *West's* Colorado Revised Statutes Annotated.

CRIME VICTIM COMPENSATION: §§24-4.1-100.1 to 24-4.1-124.

VICTIMS' RIGHTS: §24-4.1-301 and Constitutional Amendment, Art. II, §16a.
- Notice of status of case.
- Information on victim services.
- Notice of hearings and schedule changes.
- Entitled to secure waiting area to minimize contact with defendant.
- Notice of final deposition.
- Notice of right to pursue civil judgment.
- Speedy disposition right.

STATUTES OF LIMITATION:
Injury to person or sexual abuse discovery: §80-103(1)(a).
Length of time: 1 year.
Sexual abuse discovery: §13-80-103.7(1) (1992) and §13-80-108(1) (1992).
Length of time: Within 6 years after a disability has been removed for a person under disability, or within 6 years after a cause of action accrues, whichever occurs later.
Conditions: Accrual is defined as the date when "both the injury and its cause are known or should have been known by the exercise of reasonable diligence."

Connecticut

THE LAW: Connecticut General Statutes Annotated.

CRIME VICTIM COMPENSATION: §§968.54.201 to 968.54.224 and Constitutional Amendment, Art. 17.

VICTIMS' RIGHTS: §§54-202 to 54-233.
- Applies to persons who are physically injured as a result of crime.
- Police should provide victim with a card listing rights and refer victim to Office of Victim Services for assistance.
- May request information and to participate in case by informing Office of Victim Services.
- May request notice of status of case, bail decisions, plea bargain, and disposition.
- May request to be notified whenever defendant makes application to Board of Pardons or Parole, department of corrections, or sentencing judge for early release; victim to receive notice in writing, including date and place of any hearing.
- Victim has right to make oral or written impact statement.

STATUTES OF LIMITATION:
Injury to person or sexual abuse discovery: §52-577.
Length of time: 3 years
Sexual abuse discovery: §52-577d
Conditions: "Notwithstanding the provisions of section 52.577, no action to recover damages for personal injury to a minor, including emotional distress, caused by sexual abuse, sexual exploitation or sexual assault may be brought by such person later that 17 years from the date such person attains the age of majority."

Delaware

THE LAW: Delaware Code Annotated.

CRIME VICTIM COMPENSATION: Title 11, §. 9001.

VICTIMS' RIGHTS: Title 11, §§ 9401 to 9416.
- Police must give victim rights information upon contact with victim.
- Victim entitled to designate representative.
- Prosecutor must confer with victim prior to disposition of case.
- Victims are entitled to a safe waiting area which minimizes contact with defense.
- Victim entitled to be present during court proceedings on same basis as defendant.
- Disclosure of victim and family's name and address is prohibited without court order upon good cause shown.
- Victim entitled to notice of escape or release of defendant.
- Victim entitled to make impact statement prior to sentencing and parole decision, and to obtain notice of disposition.

STATUTES OF LIMITATION:
Injury to person or sexual abuse discovery: Title 10, §8119.

District of Columbia

THE LAW: District of Columbia Code.

CRIME VICTIM COMPENSATION: §§3-401 to 3-415.

VICTIMS' RIGHTS: §23-103a.
- Applies only to assault, sodomy, kidnapping, manslaughter, murder, rape, robbery, aggravated assault, and other defined crimes.
- Representative may act for deceased victim.
- Victim has right to be present at trial, if it doesn't prejudice testimony.
- Entitled to write victim impact statement which will be made part of presentence investigation report for consideration by judge prior to sentencing.
- In victim impact statement, victim can express opinion on whether defendant should be paroled.
- Victim has right to address parole hearing board on whether defendant should receive parole.

STATUTES OF LIMITATION:
Injury to person or sexual abuse discovery: §12-301(4).
Length of time: 1 year.

Florida

THE LAW: Florida Statutes. These may be found in the official books published by the State, titled "Florida Statutes," or in "West's Florida Statutes Annotated." With "Florida Statutes" a new set of books is published in odd-numbered years, with supplements printed in even-numbered years. Also, new laws may be found in a set of volumes titled "Florida Session Laws."

CRIME VICTIM COMPENSATION: Florida Statutes, §§960.01 to 960.28.

VICTIMS' RIGHTS: §960.001 and Constitutional Amendment Art I, §16.
- Requires law enforcement to provide information on victim treatment, compensation, role of victim, and how to get information on protection from intimidation.
- Victims are entitled to notice of scheduled hearings and continuances.
- Provides for "civil restitution lien" (§960.29) imposed against real and personal property and future "windfall profits" of the defendant.
- Provides for civil enforcement (§960.29) of restitution lien for a period of 20 years.

STATUTES OF LIMITATION:
Injury to person or sexual abuse discovery: §95.11(3)(o).
Length of time: 4 years.

Georgia

THE LAW: Official Code of Georgia Annotated. **CAUTION:** This is not the same as the "Georgia Code," which is an outdated set of books.

CRIME VICTIM COMPENSATION: §§27-3701 to 27-3714.

VICTIMS' RIGHTS: §§27-3901 to 27-3915.
- Applies to defined "serious crimes."
- Permits victim to have a designated representative during disability.
- Requires law enforcement to give victim notice and information on victim rights, role of victim in criminal justice proceedings, crime victim compensation, and victim services.
- Entitled to notice of arrest, release, bail hearing, and decision regarding bail.
- Entitled to secure waiting area which minimizes contact with defendant during court proceedings.
- Prohibits transmitting to defendant victim's address, phone number, or place of employment (§27-3910).
- Permits victim to express opinion on disposition, and to file objection to parole.
- Restitution can be ordered as condition of parole (§17-14-4).

STATUTES OF LIMITATION:
Injury to person or sexual abuse discovery: §9-3-33.
Length of time: 2 years.

Hawaii

THE LAW: Hawaii Revised Statutes. Ignore "Title" numbers.

CRIME VICTIM COMPENSATION: Hawaii Revised Statutes, §§ 351-1 to 351-52.

VICTIMS' RIGHTS: §§ 801D-1 to 801D-6.
- Applies to crimes and juvenile offenses; additional rights for victims of felony offenses.
- Must report crime within 3 months unless good cause present for delay.
- Entitled to notice of financial and social services available.
- Entitled to make written request for information about scheduling, changes, and final disposition.
- Victims of felony crimes entitled to receive notice of major case developments, including arrest, release, referral to prosecutor for charging, filing of charges, rejection, preliminary hearing date, grand jury date, trial, sentencing dates, and disposition.
- Entitled to secure waiting area while attending court proceedings; protection from harm or threat of harm as a result of cooperation with prosecution.
- Upon request, entitled to return of property within 10 days of its collection.
- Notice of escape, work-release, furlough, supervised release, parole, bail release, release pending appeal, and release at end of term of incarceration.

STATUTES OF LIMITATION:
Injury to person or sexual abuse discovery: §657-7.
Length of time: 2 years.

Idaho

THE LAW: Idaho Code.

CRIME VICTIM COMPENSATION: §§72-1001 to 72-1025.

VICTIMS' RIGHTS: §19-5306 and Constitutional Amendment Art. I §22.
- Applies to felonies, misdemeanors with physical injuries, sex offenses, and juvenile cases.
- Prosecutor must consult with victim.
- Entitled to be present at all case proceedings.
- Written victim impact information to be included in presentence report and victim may present orally at sentencing hearing.
- Entitled to notice of disposition of case.
- Restitution is a priority for all victims (§19-5304).
- Victim to be notified of all parole hearings and has right to present oral or written impact statement.
- Entitled to information about escape or release of defendant.

STATUTES OF LIMITATION:
Injury to person or sexual abuse discovery: §5-219(5).
Length of time: 2 years.

Illinois

THE LAW: ILLINOIS COMPILED STATUTES (ILCS)

CRIME VICTIM COMPENSATION: Ch. 740 Act 45 Sec. 45.1 to 45.20, Illinois Compiled Statutes.

VICTIMS' RIGHTS: Ch. 725 Act 120; and Constitutional Amendment: Art. I Sec. 8.1.
- Applies to violent crimes, sex offenses, misdemeanors involving bodily harm or death, certain traffic offenses, and juvenile cases.
- Notice of status of filing of charges, date, time, and place of bail.
- Entitled to information on financial and social services available.
- Employer intercession services.
- Right to a secure waiting area to minimize contact with defendant while at court proceedings.
- Right to have support person present in court.
- May request information on bail release, disposition, and appeal.
- May request to be consulted before plea offer, and nontechnical explanation of plea agreement.
- Written victim impact statement in addition to presentence investigation report, and may present at sentencing hearing.
- May request information on release, escape, transfer to mental health facility, or death of defendant.

STATUTES OF LIMITATION:
Injury to person or sexual abuse discovery: §735 ILCS 5/13-202.
Length of time: 2 years.
Injury to person or sexual abuse discovery: §735 ILCS 5/13-202.2.
Length of time: Within two years of the date the person abused discovers or through the use of reasonable diligence should discover that the act of childhood sexual abuse occurred and that the injury was caused by the childhood sexual abuse, but in no event may an action for personal injury based on childhood sexual abuse be commenced more than 12 years after the date on which the person abused attains the age of 18 years.
Conditions: If the injury is caused by 2 or more acts of childhood sexual abuse that are part of a continuing series of acts of childhood sexual abuse by the same abuser, then the discovery period under subsection is computed from the date the person abused discovers or through the use of reasonable diligence should discover (i) that the last act of childhood sexual abuse in the continuing series occurred, and (ii) that the injury was caused by any act of childhood sexual abuse in the continuing series.

Indiana

THE LAW: *West's* Annotated Indiana Code.

CRIME VICTIM COMPENSATION: §§5-2-6.1-1 to 5-2-6.1-48.

VICTIMS' RIGHTS: §33-14-9-21 and Constitutional Amendment (Nov. 96).
- Crime must be reported with 5 days unless good cause exists for delay.
- Victim must cooperate with law enforcement.
- In certain cases, victim may request diversion to victim-offender mediation program (VORP).
- Court may revoke bond if defendant threatens or harms victim.
- Right to be present at court unless court orders otherwise.
- Entitled to information on notice of all hearings and proceedings, and scheduling changes.
- Entitled to information on financial, social mental health, and legal services available to victims.
- May request restitution.

STATUTES OF LIMITATION:
Injury to person or sexual abuse discovery: §34-1-2-2(1).
Length of time: 2 years.

Iowa

THE LAW: Iowa Code Annotated.

CRIME VICTIM COMPENSATION: §§912.1 to 912.12.

VICTIMS' RIGHTS: §910A.1 to 910A.19.
- Applies to crimes and juvenile cases.
- Entitled to information on crime victim compensation.
- Police or corrections to notify victim of escape of defendant.
- County attorney required to notify victim of continuances.
- Victim impact information can be filed in writing for consideration in sentencing.
- Can submit victim impact and opinion to parole board, and has right to know disposition.
- Victim restitution request (§910.1).
- Protection for identification of child victim (§910A.13).
- Child victim entitled to have a guardian ad litem (§910A.15).

STATUTES OF LIMITATION:
Injury to person or sexual abuse discovery: §614.1(2).
Length of time: 2 years.
Injury to person or sexual abuse discovery: §614.8A
Length of time: 4 years.
Conditions: An action for damages for injury suffered as a result of sexual abuse which occurred when the injured person was a child, but not discovered until after the injured person is of the age of majority, must be brought within 4 years from the time of discovery by the injured party of both the injury and the casual relationship between the injury and the sexual abuse.

Kansas

THE LAW: Kansas Statutes Annotated. There are two publishers of Kansas Statutes Annotated, so you may find the volumes titled "Kansas Statutes Annotated, Official," or "Vernon's Kansas Statutes Annotated." Both sets have very poor indexes, and the numbering system can be confusing, so you may want to ask the librarian for assistance.

CRIME VICTIM COMPENSATION: §§74-7301 to 74-7318 and Constitutional Amendment Art. 15, §15.

VICTIMS' RIGHTS: §74-7333.
- Applies to "serious crimes" defined in statute, and includes juveniles.
- Right to notice of all public hearings, including preliminary, trial, sentencing, and expungement.

STATUTES OF LIMITATION:
Injury to person or sexual abuse discovery: §60.514(2).
Length of time: 1 year.

Kentucky

THE LAW: Kentucky Revised Statutes.

CRIME VICTIM COMPENSATION: §§346.010 to 346.190.

VICTIMS' RIGHTS: §§421.500 to 421.550.
- Applies to persons who are victims of "serious crimes" as defined, including family violence.
- At initial contact, police will give notice of emergency services, (including social and medical), community treatment, and crime victim compensation available to victims.
- Police will explain methods of protection from intimidation, the criminal justice process, and provide information on arrest.
- Speedy trial in child sexual abuse cases.
- Entitled to prompt return of property and employer intercession.
- Prosecutor will consult with victim prior to dismissal, release, negotiating plea, or pretrial diversion disposition.
- On request, victim entitled to notice of hearings, release of defendant, filing of charges, and trial date.
- Victim entitled to make a victim impact statement and comment on sentence to be included in pre-sentence investigation report for consideration at sentencing, and may request notification and present victim impact information at parole hearing.

STATUTES OF LIMITATION:
Injury to person or sexual abuse discovery: §413.140(1)(a).
Length of time: 1 year.

Louisiana

THE LAW: *West's* L.S.A. (for Louisiana Statutes Annotated). This set of books are divided into sets of volumes according to subject, such as "Revised Statutes," "Civil Code," "Criminal Procedure," etc., so be sure you have the correct set.

CRIME VICTIM COMPENSATION: §§46.1802 to 46.1822.

VICTIMS' RIGHTS: §§46.1841 to 46.1844.
- Applies to felonies, misdemeanors, and juvenile cases.
- Must report within 72 hours of the crime, except for good cause shown.
- Entitled to brochure on rights, including availability of crime victim compensation, treatment, counseling, role of victim, stages of criminal process, and protection from intimidation.
- Law enforcement must provide private interviewing rooms.
- On request, entitled to notice of arrest, bail release.
- Speedy trial right.
- Law enforcement must provide private interviewing rooms.
- Prosecutor must confer with victim prior to disposition and discuss sentencing alternatives.
- Victim impact statement for consideration in sentencing hearing.
- Restitution as a condition of probation or parole.
- Notification of escape or release of prisoner.

STATUTES OF LIMITATION:
Injury to person or sexual abuse discovery: Civil Code §3492.
Length of time: 1 year.

Maine

THE LAW: Maine Revised Statutes Annotated.

CRIME VICTIM COMPENSATION: Title 5, §§ 3360 to 3360-L.

VICTIMS' RIGHTS: Title 15, § 6101.
- Applies to serious crimes, sex offenses, and domestic violence.
- Prosecutor shall notify victim of victim compensation availability.
- Victim entitled to notice of plea agreement before it is entered into court.
- Notification of time and place of trial.
- Written victim impact information for consideration in sentencing, and oral presentation at hearing.
- Prosecutor must inform court of victim's position on plea or sentence.
- Restitution is mandatory (Title 17A, §§54.1322 to 54.1330).

STATUTES OF LIMITATION:
Injury to person or sexual abuse discovery: Title 14, §753.
Length of time: 2 years.
Injury to person or sexual abuse discovery: Title 14, §752-C
Conditions: "Actions based upon sexual intercourse or a sexual act...with a person under the age of majority must be commenced within 12 years after the cause of action accrues, or within 6 years of the time the person discovers or reasonably should have discovered the harm, whichever occurs later."

Maryland

THE LAW: Annotated Code of Maryland. These books are arranged by subject, such as "Courts & Judicial Procedure," "Family Law," etc., so be sure you have the correct volume.

CRIME VICTIM COMPENSATION: Article 26.A; Sec. 1 - 18.

VICTIMS' RIGHTS: Art. 27, §761 and Constitutional Amendment Art. 47.
- Notice includes information on crime victim compensation and social services.
- Entitled to separate waiting area to minimize contact with defendant.
- On request, kept informed of scheduled hearing and continuances.
- Speedy trial right.
- Right to make a victim impact statement.
- May request restitution.
- Notice of parole hearing and release in advance; and escape or furlough.
- Presumption of restitution (Art. 27, §640).

STATUTES OF LIMITATION:
Injury to person or sexual abuse discovery: Courts & Judicial Procedure §5-105.
Length of time: 1 year.

Massachusetts

THE LAW: Annotated Laws of Massachusetts.

CRIME VICTIM COMPENSATION: Chapter 258C, §§1 to 13.

VICTIMS' RIGHTS: Ch. 258B, §§1 to 10.
- Applies to crimes and juvenile cases.
- Entitled to protection from intimidation and methods.
- Entitled to secure waiting area to minimize contact with defendant during court appearance.
- Entitled to information from prosecutor on disposition, release of defendant, scheduling, and continuances.
- May request restitution.
- Entitled to information from prosecutor on disposition.

STATUTES OF LIMITATION:
Injury to person or sexual abuse discovery: Ch. 260, §4.
Length of time: 3 years.

Michigan

THE LAW: Michigan Compiled Laws Annotated (abbreviated "M.C.L.A."), or Michigan Statutes Annotated (abbreviated "M.S.A."). Michigan has sets of books by two separate publishers, each with its own numbering system. Both have a cross-reference index to the other set. The references below give the cites to both sets. Ignore the volume and "Chapter" numbers.

CRIME VICTIM COMPENSATION: Michigan Compiled Laws Annotated, §§18.351 to 18.368; Michigan Statutes Annotated, §3.372(1) to §3.372(18).

VICTIMS' RIGHTS: M.C.L.A. §780.751; M.S.A. §28.1287; and Constitutional Amendment: Art. I Sec. 24.
- Applies to felony crimes and juvenile cases.
- Law enforcement must give written notice of rights, including phone number and address of police and prosecutor.
- On evidence of threat to victim, prosecutor can seek to revoke bail.
- 7 days after arraignment and 24 hours before preliminary hearing, prosecutor must give notice in writing of rights and procedures for protection from intimidation, and provide name and contact of assigned prosecutor.
- Victim entitled to safe waiting area while at court; entitled to be present on same basis as defendant.
- Prosecutor must consult with victim prior to disposition.
- Victim privacy for address or other private information.
- Restitution mandatory (M.C.L.A., §780.766; M.S.A. §28.1287).
- Oral or written victim impact statement prior to sentencing.
- Entitled to notice of escape or release.

STATUTES OF LIMITATION:
Injury to person or sexual abuse discovery: M.C.L.A., §600.5805(2); M.S.A., §27A-5805.
Length of time: 2 years.

Minnesota

THE LAW: Minnesota Statutes Annotated.

CRIME VICTIM COMPENSATION: §§611A.51 to 611A.68.

VICTIMS' RIGHTS: §§611A.01 to 611A.06.
- Crimes, includes local ordinance violations if bodily harm to victim; juvenile & certain traffic offenses.
- Law enforcement must deliver notice of rights to victim.
- Can request law enforcement to withhold identity in public records.
- May not be compelled to state address of home or business in open court.
- Entitled to notice of plea agreement and input prior to pretrial diversion.
- Victim impact statement for consideration in sentencing.
- Restitution request (§611A.04).
- Notice of escape or release.

STATUTES OF LIMITATION:
Injury to person or sexual abuse discovery: §541.07(1).
Length of time: 2 years.
Injury to person or sexual abuse discovery: §541.073
Length of time: An action for personal injury caused by sexual abuse must be commenced within 6 years of the time the plaintiff knew or had reason to know the injury was caused by the sexual abuse.
Conditions: In a cause of action for damages commenced against a person who caused the plaintiff's personal injury either by (1) committing sexual abuse against the plaintiff, or (2) negligently permitting sexual abuse against the plaintiff to occur: The plaintiff need not establish which act in a continuous series of sexual abuse acts by the defendant caused the injury. The knowledge of a parent or guardian may not be imputed to a minor.

Mississippi

THE LAW: Mississippi Code 1972 Annotated.

CRIME VICTIM COMPENSATION: §§99-41-1 to 41-29.

VICTIMS' RIGHTS: §99-36-5.
- Applies to all crimes and juvenile cases.
- Must report crime within 5 days to be eligible for rights, unless good cause shown.
- Police must notify of defendant's escape or release from jail.
- Same right as defendant to be present in court.
- Restitution request (99-37-1 -37-25).

STATUTES OF LIMITATION:
Injury to person or sexual abuse discovery: §15-1-35.
Length of time: 1 year.

Missouri

THE LAW: *Vernon's* Annotated Missouri Statutes.

CRIME VICTIM COMPENSATION: §§595.010 to 595.070.

VICTIMS' RIGHTS: §§595.200 to 595.209 and Constitutional Amendment Art. I, §32.
- Applies to crimes against persons.
- Right to be informed of status of case.
- Right to notice of defendant's release on bond.
- Entitled to a secure waiting area which minimizes contact with defendant.
- Return of property within 5 days of request.
- Right to information on restitution [§595.209 (11)].

STATUTES OF LIMITATION:
Injury to person or sexual abuse discovery: §516:140.
Length of time: 2 years.
Injury to person or sexual abuse discovery: §537.046.
Conditions: In any civil action for recovery of damages suffered as a result of childhood sexual abuse, the time for commencement of the action must be within 5 years of the date the plaintiff attains the age of 18, or within 3 years of the date the plaintiff discovers or reasonably should have discovered that the injury or illness was caused by child sexual abuse, whichever later occurs.

Montana

THE LAW: Montana Code Annotated. The code sections are in a set of black, soft-cover volumes. The annotations are in a separate set of loose-leaf binders.

CRIME VICTIM COMPENSATION: Montana Code Annotated, §§53.9.101 to 53.9.133.

VICTIMS' RIGHTS: §§46-24-101 to 24-213.
- Applies to felonies, misdemeanors with bodily harm, or the family of homicide victim.
- Attorney General required to provide a form for notice.
- Prosecution must consult on plea before disposition.
- Upon request, felony victim can submit a statement to parole board.
- Entitled to reasonable notice of release on furlough, work release, or community program.

STATUTES OF LIMITATION:
Injury to person or sexual abuse discovery: §27-2-204(3).
Length of time: 2 years.
Injury to person and/or sexual abuse discovery: §27-2-216 (1991).
Conditions: An action based on intentional conduct brought by a person for recovery of damages for injury suffered as a result of childhood sexual abuse must be commenced not later that: (a) 3 years after the act of childhood sexual abuse that is alleged to have caused the injury; or (b) 3 years after the plaintiff discovers or reasonably should have discovered that the injury was caused by the act of childhood sexual abuse.

Nebraska

THE LAW: Revised Statutes of Nebraska.

CRIME VICTIM COMPENSATION: §§81-1801 to 81-1842.

VICTIMS' RIGHTS: §§81-1843 to 81-1850.
- Applies to defined crimes (§29-119).
- Entitled to a copy of police report, arrest warrant, and indictment.
- Entitled to information on status of case and hearings.
- Right to testify before parole board or submit statement.
- Right to notice of disposition.
- Entitled to notice of release, escape, or discharge.
- Victim name and identifying information is not public information.

STATUTES OF LIMITATION:
Injury to person or sexual abuse discovery: §25-208.
Length of time: 1 year.

Nevada

THE LAW: Nevada Revised Statutes Annotated.

CRIME VICTIM COMPENSATION: §§217.010 to 217.270 and Constitutional Amendment Art. I §8.

VICTIMS' RIGHTS: §178.569.
- Applies to victims or relative of victims.
- Police will investigate and take measures to protect victim from intimidation.
- Entitled to notice of hearings and schedule changes.
- Entitled to make one telephone call.
- On written request, entitled to notice in writing.
- Court will provide secure waiting area to minimize contact with defendant.
- Entitled to prompt return of property and witness fee information.
- Notice of release from custody, and disposition.
- Sex crimes victims entitled to support person in court.

STATUTES OF LIMITATION:
Injury to person or sexual abuse discovery: §11.190-4(c).
Length of time: 2 years.
Injury to person or sexual abuse discovery: §11.215
Conditions: An action to recover damages for an injury to a person arising from the sexual abuse of the plaintiff which occurred when the plaintiff was less than 18 years of age must be commenced within 3 years after the plaintiff; (a) reaches 18 years of age; or (b) discovers or reasonably should have discovered that his injury was caused by the sexual abuse, whichever occurs later.

New Hampshire

THE LAW: New Hampshire Revised Statutes Annotated.

CRIME VICTIM COMPENSATION: §§21M:8-f to 21M: 8-1.

VICTIMS' RIGHTS: §21M:8-k.
- Applies to victims of felonies, and immediate family members of a minor, incompetent, or homicide victim.
- Entitled to information about criminal justice process, victim assistance, social services, financial services, and crime victim compensation.
- Right to prompt return of property.
- Notice of proceedings and scheduling.
- Same right as defendant to attend court.
- Right to confer with prosecutor and be consulted regarding disposition, including plea bargain.
- Oral or written victim impact statement to be considered in sentencing or plea agreement.
- Notice of change in status, escape or release of prisoner, date of parole hearing, and oral or written victim impact statement; notice of disposition.
- Notice and right to attend appeal proceedings.

STATUTES OF LIMITATION:
Injury to person or sexual abuse discovery: §508:4.
Length of time: 3 years.

New Jersey

THE LAW: NJSA (for New Jersey Statutes Annotated).

CRIME VICTIM COMPENSATION: §§52:4B-1 to 52:4B-33.

VICTIMS' RIGHTS: §§52:4B-34 to 4B-38 and Constitutional Amendment Art. I, ¶22.
- Applies to all crimes.
- Entitled to at least one phone call.
- Notice of 24-hour hotline.
- Victim impact statement to prosecutor prior to decision of whether formal charges will be filed.
- In-person statement directly to judge concerning impact.
- Restitution request and information §52:4B-36.
- Entitled to parole consideration of victim impact.
- Notice of escape or release.

STATUTES OF LIMITATION:
Injury to person or sexual abuse discovery: §2A:14-2.
Length of time: 2 years.

New Mexico

THE LAW: New Mexico Statutes 1978 Annotated.

CRIME VICTIM COMPENSATION: Chapter 325.

VICTIMS' RIGHTS: §31-24-1; and Constitutional Amendment: Art. 2, Sec. 24.
- Applies to defined crimes (includes: arson, aggravated assault, aggravated battery, murder, voluntary and involuntary manslaughter, kidnapping, criminal sexual penetration, and criminal sexual contact of a minor, homicide, and great bodily harm by vehicle).
- Victim includes family representative where victim is minor, incompetent, or deceased.
- Must report crime within 5 days or have good cause; rights are effective upon filing charges.
- Police provide written contact and status notice, including name and phone number of prosecutor.
- May appoint a representative.
- 7 days after filing charge, prosecutor must provide victim with written rights.
- Right to be present at court proceedings.
- Right to notice of escape.

STATUTES OF LIMITATION:
Injury to person or sexual abuse discovery: §37-1-8.
Length of time: 3 years.

New York

THE LAW: McKinney's Consolidated Laws of New York Annotated. These books are divided into subjects, such as "Penal Law," "Domestic Relations Law," etc., so be sure you have the correctly titled volume.

CRIME VICTIM COMPENSATION: N.Y. Exec. Law Ch. 620.

VICTIMS' RIGHTS: N.Y. Exec. Law Ch. 640 to 649.
- Applies to violent felonies, and property crimes over a certain amount.
- Police must interview victim privately.
- Police must provide sex crimes victims with notice of nearest rape crisis center.
- Entitled to secure waiting area to minimize contact with defendant during attendance at court proceedings.
- Entitled to provide victim impact information for consideration in sentencing.
- Right to restitution (Penal Law, §60.27).

STATUTES OF LIMITATION:
Injury to person or sexual abuse discovery: N.Y. CIV. PRAC. L. & R. §215.
Length of time: 1 year.

North Carolina

THE LAW: General Statutes of North Carolina. Lawyers and judge commonly refer to these as the "North Carolina General Statutes," although that is not the title as printed on the cover of the volumes.

CRIME VICTIM COMPENSATION: North Carolina General Statutes, §§15B-1 to 15B-25.

VICTIMS' RIGHTS: §15A-824 and 15A- 825 and Constitutional Amendment.
- Applies to serious misdemeanors, felonies, and juvenile cases.
- Entitled to request prosecutor to object to questions regarding victim's home address.
- Entitled to information on protection from harm.
- Same right to be present in court as defendant.
- On request, entitled to make a victim impact statement for consideration in sentencing.
- May request information on escape or release of prisoner.

STATUTES OF LIMITATION:
Injury to person or sexual abuse discovery: §1-52(5).
Length of time: 3 years.

North Dakota

THE LAW: North Dakota Century Code Annotated.

CRIME VICTIM COMPENSATION: §§54-23.4-01 to 54-23.4-18.

VICTIMS' RIGHTS: §§12.1-34-.01 to 12.1-34-.05.
- Applies to felonies, specified misdemeanors, and juvenile cases.
- Right to be informed of status of investigation.
- Right to notice of charges filed, procedures followed, pretrial release and conditions, participation in court (advance notice), and continuances.
- Entitled to information on social services.
- Entitled to secure waiting area, prompt return of property.
- May not be compelled to testify as to address, phone number, or other personal information without court approval.
- Right to be present in court, subject to rules of evidence.
- Written victim impact statement; comment on sentence and restitution; oral statement at judge's discretion.
- Notice of disposition, release, escape, work-release, or community or mental health release; right to have impact statement presented in parole and pardon procedures.

STATUTES OF LIMITATION:
Injury to person or sexual abuse discovery: §28-01-18.
Length of time: 2 years.

Ohio

THE LAW: *Page's* Ohio Revised Code Annotated. Look for the title number, which will be the same as the first two numbers of the section number listed below. For example, to find §3103.05, you would look for the volume marked "Title 31."

CRIME VICTIM COMPENSATION: §§2743.51 to 2743.72; 2743.121; 2743.191; and 2743.20.

VICTIMS' RIGHTS: §§2930.01 to 2930.19; and Constitution, Art I, Sec. 10a.
- Applies to any felony and other defined crimes.
- Victim may designate representative; court may appoint representative for minor, incapacitated, or deceased victim.
- Police must provide written information about rights, social, and financial services, and a contact number.
- Notice of arrest and release information; prosecutor can request revocation of bond if victim threatened or harmed.
- Notice of scheduled hearings; victim may object to delay; prosecutor must confer with victim before dismissing charge or entry of plea; victim entitled to name of case and case number.
- Right to be present in court, subject to rules of evidence; right to secure waiting area to minimize contact with defendant.
- Victim cannot be compelled to testify as to address, phone number, or similar identifying information.
- Victim impact statement (written or oral) includes restitution and comment on sentence and release.
- Notice of incarceration, escape, release, death.

STATUTES OF LIMITATION:
Injury to person or sexual abuse discovery: §2305.11(a); §2305.10.
Length of time: 1 year or 2 years if bodily injury.

Oklahoma

THE LAW: Oklahoma Statutes Annotated.

CRIME VICTIM COMPENSATION: Title 21, §§142-1 to 142-18.

VICTIMS' RIGHTS: Title 19, §215-33 and Constitutional Amendment Art II §34.
- Applies to violent crimes and juvenile cases.
- Includes family members of homicide victims, and witnesses to crime.
- Information on protection from harm and methods.
- Right to secure waiting area while attending court proceedings.
- Notice of financial and social services; employer intercession.
- Entitled to notice of scheduled hearings and continuances.
- Information on plea agreement.
- Victim impact statement for consideration by court in sentencing.
- Information about reversal of conviction.

STATUTES OF LIMITATION:
Injury to person or sexual abuse discovery: Title 12 §95(4).
Length of time: 1 year.

Oregon

THE LAW: Oregon Revised Statutes Annotated.

CRIME VICTIM COMPENSATION: §§147.005 to 147.375.

VICTIMS' RIGHTS: §§147.405 to 147.415 and Constitutional Amendment Art. I.
- Declares victims are entitled to fair and impartial treatment.
- Victims are to be protected at each stage of proceedings.

STATUTES OF LIMITATION:
Injury to person or sexual abuse discovery: Title 12, §110.
Length of time: 2 years.

Pennsylvania

THE LAW: *Purdon's* Pennsylvania Consolidated Statutes Annotated.

CRIME VICTIM COMPENSATION: Title 71 §§180-7 to 180.720.

VICTIMS' RIGHTS: Title 71 §§180-9.3 to 180-9.11.
- Applies to specified crimes.
- Specific criminal justice personnel are responsible to provide basic victim's information, including information on crime victim compensation, in writing within 24 hours of contact.
- Victim's address and phone number cannot be disseminated to other than police, prosecutor, and corrections without consent of victim (Title 71 §180-9.10).
- In personal injury crimes, notice of arrest by police and notice of escape from custody.
- In personal injury crimes, burglary, or certain vehicle crimes, the right to comment prior to the prosecutor's decision to reduce or drop a charge, or accept or change a plea.
- May make a victim impact statement to court for consideration in sentencing; right to restitution, if possible.
- May provide victim impact information for pardon or parole consideration.
- Entitled to information on release, individual work-release, furlough, community treatment, escape, or transfer to mental health facility.

STATUTES OF LIMITATION:
Injury to person or sexual abuse discovery: Title 42, §5524(1).
Length of time: 2 years.

Rhode Island

THE LAW: General Laws of Rhode Island. Ignore "Title" and "Chapter" numbers.

CRIME VICTIM COMPENSATION: General Laws of Rhode Island, §§12-25-1 to 12-25-14.

VICTIMS' RIGHTS: §§12-28-1 to 12-28-10; and Constitution, Article I, Section 23.
- Victim must make "timely report" and cooperate with police.
- Police to notify victim of status at least every 3 months.
- Family member designated in death or incapacity of victim.
- Right to notice of arraignment and bail release, and court proceedings at which victim's presence is required.
- In misdemeanor cases, right to address court on impact and disposition at pretrial conference, at judge's discretion.
- Notice of available methods of protection from intimidation, and secure waiting area to minimize contact with defendant while at court.
- Notice of available intercession, witness fees, return of property, and financial and social services.
- In felony cases, right to address court on victim impact and sentencing, and victim impact for parole consideration.
- Notice of disposition and release from incarceration.
- Right to request restitution.

STATUTES OF LIMITATION:
Injury to person or sexual abuse discovery: §9-1-14.
Length of time: 3 years.

South Carolina

THE LAW: Code of Laws of South Carolina.

CRIME VICTIM COMPENSATION: Code of Laws of South Carolina, §§16-3-1110 to 16-3-1340.

VICTIMS' RIGHTS: §§16-3-1510 to 16-3-1560 and Constitutional Amendment Art. I §24.
- Applies to any victim who has physical, emotional, or financial harm as a result of crime.
- Young, elderly, or handicapped victim entitled to special consideration and attention.
- Entitled to freedom from intimidation and secure waiting area while at court; police to provide transportation to court and physical protection in courthouse.
- Information about financial and social services, witness fee, crime victim compensation availability, and civil remedies including lien on profits.
- Notice of release on bail and recommendations made, procedures, hearings, and continuances in time to attend.
- Right to attend court (subject to judge's discretion); right to have counsel represent victim in cases involving victim's reputation.
- Entitled to confer with prosecutor and plea information.
- Right to present written or oral victim impact statement to judge for consideration in sentencing; restitution is mandatory (§17-25-322).
- Notice of disposition and release from incarceration.

STATUTES OF LIMITATION:
Injury to person or sexual abuse discovery: §15-3-550.
Length of time: 2 years.

South Dakota

THE LAW: South Dakota Codified Laws.

CRIME VICTIM COMPENSATION: §§23A-28B-1 to 23A-28B-44.

VICTIMS' RIGHTS: §§23A-28C-1 to 23A-28C-5.
- Applies to crimes of violence, certain vehicular crimes, and domestic violence.
- Family member designated as representative for deceased victim.
- Victim must notify prosecutor to participate and provide address; entitled to name of prosecutor assigned to case and right to be prepared as a witness.
- Notice of scheduled bail hearings, release, and right to testify on danger (§23A28C-1(3)).
- Notice of charges and elements, and dates of preliminary hearing and trial.
- Information on protection from intimidation.
- Right to be present in court, subject to judge's discretion.
- Victim input in plea negotiation and impact information (oral or written) as well as comment on appropriate sentence to court; written impact information for consideration in parole or commutation.
- Restitution may be requested in sentence of probation or incarceration.
- Notice of disposition and release from incarceration.

STATUTES OF LIMITATION:
Injury to person or sexual abuse discovery: §15-2-15.
Length of time: 2 years.
Injury to person and/or sexual abuse discovery: §26-10-25
Conditions: Any civil action based on intentional conduct brought by any person for recovery of damages for injury suffered as a result of childhood sexual abuse must be commenced within 3 years of the act alleged to have caused the injury or condition, or 3 years of the time the victim discovered or reasonably should have discovered that the injury or condition was caused by the act, whichever period expires later.

Tennessee

THE LAW: Tennessee Code Annotated.

CRIME VICTIM COMPENSATION: §§29-13-101 to 29-13-118.

VICTIMS' RIGHTS: §§40-38-101 to 40-38-208.
- Applies to all crimes.
- Information on procedures and stages of criminal justice process.
- Priority scheduling of crimes against person.
- Information on recovery of property and crime victim compensation.
- In cases of violent crime involving death or serious injury, notice of bail release; in other cases, may request information.
- Notice of time, date, and location of hearings; and continuances.
- Information on plea negotiations and agreements; in cases of violent crime involving death or serious injury, right to give impact statement to court and to speak at parole hearings.
- In cases of felony involving death or injury to victim, victim impact statement becomes part of pre-sentence investigation report.
- Information on release, appeals process, restitution rights, and civil process rights.

STATUTES OF LIMITATION:
Injury to person or sexual abuse discovery: §28-3-104.
Length of time: 1 year.

Texas

THE LAW: *Vernon's* Texas Codes Annotated. These books are divided into subjects, such as "Civil Practice & Remedies," "Family," "Probate," etc., so be sure you have the correctly titled volume.

CRIME VICTIM COMPENSATION: Code of Criminal Procedure §§56.31 to 56.61.

VICTIMS' RIGHTS: §§56.01 to 56.11; and Constitution, Article I, Section 30.
- Applies to crimes involving bodily injury or death; includes sexual assault, kidnapping, and aggravated robbery.
- Victim includes guardian or close relative of deceased.
- Right to adequate protection from harm and threats.
- At initial contact, police to provide written information on proceedings, bail, pleas, restitution available, appeal, and crime victim compensation.
- Consideration of bail must include safety of victim.
- Within 10 days of filing charges, prosecutor to provide notice of rights to victim, including right to request notice of time, date, location of hearings and continuances.
- Entitled to secure waiting area while attending court, prompt return of property, and employer intercession.
- Right to be present in court, subject to judge's discretion.
- Entitled to make victim impact statement to probation office for inclusion in presentence investigative report.
- Notice of parole procedures.

STATUTES OF LIMITATION:
Injury to person or sexual abuse discovery: Civil Practice & Remedies, §16.003.
Length of time: 2 years.

Utah

THE LAW: Utah Code Annotated.

CRIME VICTIM COMPENSATION: §§63-63-1 to 63-63-31.

VICTIMS' RIGHTS: §§77-38-1 to 77-38-14; and Constitution, Article I, Section 28.
- Applies to felony crimes and juvenile cases.
- Permits designation of representative for victim.
- Within 7 days of filing felony, prosecutor must provide initial notice (oral and written) about electing to receive further notices, including notice of "important court hearings."
- Subject to rules of evidence, victim has right to be present at important court hearings and to be heard at defendant's initial appearance on issues related to release.
- Court must consider victim's interests in continuances (§77-38-7).
- Can exercise victim impact statement through oral, written, audiotape, or videotape, to be included in presentence investigative report; where number of victims exceeds 5, court may limit oral statements to a representative number of victims.
- Board of pardons and parole must provide notice of parole procedures and hearings.

STATUTES OF LIMITATION:
Injury to person or sexual abuse discovery: §78-12-29(4).
Length of time: 1 year.
Injury to person and/or sexual abuse discovery: §78-12-25.1
Conditions: (1) A person must file a civil action for intentional or negligent sexual abuse suffered as a child: (a) within 4 years after the person attains the age of 18 years; or (b) if a person discovers sexual abuse only after attaining the age of 18 years, that person may bring a civil action for such sexual abuse within 4 years after discovery of the sexual abuse, whichever period expires later. (2) The victim need not establish which act in a series of continuing sexual abuse incidents caused the injury complained of. (3) The knowledge of a custodial parent or guardian shall not be imputed to a person under the age of 18 years.

Vermont

THE LAW: Vermont Statutes Annotated. Ignore "Chapter" numbers.

CRIME VICTIM COMPENSATION: Title 13, §§5351 to 5359.

VICTIMS' RIGHTS: Title 1, §§5301 to 5307.
- Applies to crimes involving injury or death, including juvenile cases.
- Victim includes family of deceased, minor, or incompetent victim; also applies to "affected persons."
- Crime must be reported to law enforcement.
- Information on level of protection available, witness fees, and restitution available.
- Entitled to short-term counseling, and referrals.
- Notice of financial, social services, prompt return of property, and employer intercession.
- Entitled to transportation to and from court where necessary.
- Except in juvenile cases, entitled to timely notice of hearings, continuances, final disposition, release and escape, and release on bail.

STATUTES OF LIMITATION:
Injury to person or sexual abuse discovery: Title 12, §512.
Length of time: 3 years.
Injury to person or sexual abuse discovery: Title 12, §522 (1991) & Title 12, §560

Conditions: A civil action brought by any person for recovery of damages for injury suffered as a result of childhood sexual abuse must be commenced within 6 years of the act alleged to have caused the injury or condition, or within 6 years of the time the victim discovered that the injury or condition was caused by that act, whichever period expires later. The victim need not establish which act in a series of continuing sexual abuse or exploitation incidents caused the injury. If a complaint is filed alleging an act of childhood sexual abuse which occurred more than 6 years prior to the date the action is commenced, the complaint must immediately be sealed by the clerk of the court. The complaint must remain sealed until the answer is served or, if the defendant files a motion to dismiss under Rule 12(b) of the Vermont Rules of Civil Procedures, until the court rules on that motion. If the complaint is dismissed, the complaint and any related papers or pleadings will remain sealed. Any hearing held in connection with the motion to dismiss must be in camera (in private, usually in the judge's chambers). Related statute: When a person entitled to bring an action for damages as a result of childhood sexual abuse is unable to commence the action as a direct result of the damages caused by the sexual abuse, the period during which the person is incapacitated will not be taken as a part of the time limited for commencement of the lawsuit.

Virginia

THE LAW: Code of Virginia 1950. Ignore "Chapter" numbers.

CRIME VICTIM COMPENSATION: §§19.2-368.1 to 19.2-368.18.

VICTIMS' RIGHTS: §§19.2-11.01 to 19.2-11.04 and Constitutional Amendment Art. I §8-A.
- Applies to all persons suffering harm as a result of felony or other defined crimes (includes assault and battery).
- Information about social and financial services, crime victim compensation, return of property, employer intercession, and right to interpreter.
- Notice of judicial proceedings and continuances.
- Information on intimidation and protection available; right to separate waiting area to minimize contact with defendant.
- Victim's address, phone number, or similar private information is confidential unless the court orders otherwise.
- Written victim impact statement, to present to court (subject to rules of evidence) for consideration in sentencing.
- Notice of escape or release of prisoner.

STATUTES OF LIMITATION:
Injury to person or sexual abuse discovery: §8.01-243(a).
Length of time: 2 years.
Injury to person and/or sexual abuse discovery: §8.01-249(6).
Conditions: In actions for injury to the person resulting from sexual abuse occurring during the infancy or incompetency of the person (whatever the theory of recovery), when the fact of the injury and its casual connection to the sexual abuse is first communicated to the person by licensed physician, psychologist, or clinical psychologist. However, no such action may be brought more than 10 years after the later of (i) the last act by the same perpetrator which was part of a common scheme of plan of abuse, or (ii) removal of the disability of infancy or incompetency.

Washington

THE LAW: *West's* Revised Code of Washington Annotated.

CRIME VICTIM COMPENSATION: §§7.68.070 to 7.68.340.

VICTIMS' RIGHTS: §7.69.020; and Constitution, Article II, Section 35.
- Applies to felonies and misdemeanors.
- Sexual crime or violent crime victims receive written statement of rights upon reporting crime, with crime victim/witness program information.
- Sexual or violent crime victims entitled to have crime victim advocate present at interviews.
- Information about return of property, final disposition and witness fees, employer intercession, and victim assistance.
- Notice of hearings and continuances including time, date, and location of trial and sentencing, and right to be present in court.
- Right to protection from harm or threats; safe waiting area to minimize defendant contact.
- Victim impact statement (written) included in presentence investigative report; oral presentation at sentencing hearing.
- Restitution is mandatory, unless court orders otherwise [7.69.030(15)].

STATUTES OF LIMITATION:
Injury to person or sexual abuse discovery: §4.16.100.
Length of time: 2 years.
Conditions: All claims or causes of action based on intentional conduct brought by any person for recovery of damages for injury suffered as a result of childhood sexual abuse must be commenced within the later of the following periods: (a) within 3 years of the act alleged to have caused the injury or condition; (b) within 3 years of the time the victim discovered or reasonably should have discovered that the injury or condition was caused by said act; or (c) within 3 years of the time the victim discovered that the act caused the injury for which the claim is brought; provided, that the time limit for commencement of an action is tolled for a child until the child reaches the age of 18 years.

West Virginia

THE LAW: West Virginia Code.

CRIME VICTIM COMPENSATION: West Virginia Code, §§14-2A-1 to 14-2A-27.

VICTIMS' RIGHTS: §§61-11A-1 to 61-11A-8.
- Applies to any felony.
- Victim includes family representative for deceased victim.
- Police to provide information about rights, role of victim and procedures, and crisis, social, and financial services.
- Prosecutor to provide steps available for intimidation protection.
- Notice of arrest, initial appearance, release on bail, hearings and scheduling changes, entry of plea, trial, and sentencing.
- Prosecutor must consult victim of a serious crime regarding disposition of case, release on bail, and plea, diversion program.
- In cases involving injury to victim, impact statement (written) must be included in presentence investigative report; in child victim cases, recommendations on effect of disposition on victim; oral victim impact to court for consideration in sentencing.
- Notice of escape or release of prisoner.
- Restitution is mandatory (§61-11A-4).

STATUTES OF LIMITATION:
Injury to person or sexual abuse discovery: §55-2-12(b).
Length of time: 2 years.

Wisconsin

THE LAW: *West's* Wisconsin Statutes Annotated. Ignore "Chapter" numbers.

CRIME VICTIM COMPENSATION: §§949.001 to 949.18.

VICTIMS' RIGHTS: §§950.01 to 950.08; and Constitution, Article I, Section 9m.
- Applies to crimes and juvenile cases.
- Victim includes family of homicide victim.
- Crime must be reported to authorities.
- Information about rights, social and financial services, witness fees, and employer intercession.
- Notice of bail release information in felony cases.
- Notice of hearings, continuances, and final disposition.
- Entitled to protection from harm and threats; right to secure waiting area to minimize contact with defendant.
- Victim impact statement and input into parole decisions.
- Notice of community release or parole.

STATUTES OF LIMITATION:
Injury to person or sexual abuse discovery: §893.57.
Length of time: 2 years.

Wyoming

THE LAW: Wyoming Statutes Annotated.

CRIME VICTIM COMPENSATION: §§1-40-101 to 1-40-119.

VICTIMS' RIGHTS: §1-40-201.
- Applies to all crimes.
- Police provide information about rights, social and financial services, interpreter/translator, return of property, employer intercession, and a contact number of officer assigned to case.
- Information on right to be free from intimidation and secure waiting area to minimize contact with defendant.
- Notice of status of investigation and release of defendant.
- Entitled to name and phone number of prosecutor assigned to case.
- Notice of scheduled hearings, disposition, sentencing, imprisonment, and release.
- Same right as defendant to be present in court and to participate.
- Victim impact statement (written) included in presentence report and oral victim impact statement presented at sentence hearing.
- Notice of escape, release, or parole conditions.

STATUTES OF LIMITATION:
Injury to person or sexual abuse discovery: §1-3-105(v)(b),(c).
Length of time: 1 year.

The victim's rights laws of every state differ, but all are found in the state statutes or codes, which are listed in Appendix B. To find your state's laws:

1.   Contact your local police department for brochures or other information.
2.   Contact your local prosecutor's office for copies of relevant laws, or speak to any available victim-witness personnel.
3.   Check with your State Attorney General's Office for a victim's or crime bureau or division.
4.   Do some legal research of your own.

Doing your own research means visiting a library. A large public library may carry legal/government books, but you may need to visit a law library in order to find updated copies of your state's legal statutes or codes. The actual title of the book is very important, so bring the relevant page from your state found in Appendix B.

Contact the closest appropriate library to determine hours and location. The reference librarians can help you find the set of books you need. Once you find the statute or code books, look for the section numbers listed in Appendix B for your state to find the exact laws. Some states have passed constitutional amendments for crime victims, which may be found in the Constitutional volume of the same state statutes or code. See the beginning of Appendix B for more information on locating and using statute or code books. Be sure to look for the most current supplement, as the laws are frequently changed.

Many victim's rights laws are found within a chapter or section of the state's criminal code. The criminal code will include the names, definitions, and elements of the various criminal offenses in your state. If you are interested in finding your specific crime and you don't have a statute or code citation, look in the index volume under the name of your crime (e.g., "assault and battery" or "aggravated assault"), or look in the index of the criminal code chapter or volume. The index will give you the statute or code section number.

Often, the statute or code books include case "annotations," which are summaries of various appellate court decisions that have interpreted and explained the laws.

The entire appellate court decisions are printed in state and regional "case reporters." These are sets of books that contain the full written opinions of the appellate courts. To find a case that is listed in the annotations, carefully copy down the case name and the numbers which follow exactly, or make a copy of the page with the case annotation on it. Next, find out where the case reporters are in the library. Many reporters have two or more "series" (i.e., instead of continuing to number the volumes, they started a second series which begins with volume 1). Also, there may be more than one reporter in which the same case can be found. Each state publishes a reporter of its cases, and there are also regional reporters which combine cases from several states in the same geographical area (as in the example below). Ask your reference librarian for assistance. The citation often looks as follows:

People v. Wheeler, 216 Ill. App.3d 609, 575 N.E.2d 1326 (1992)

| ↑ | ↑ | ↑ | ↑ |
| Name of case | State case reporter citation | Regional reporter citation | Year published |

Once you find the proper state or regional reporter, the case is found using the following method:

216	Ill. App.	3d	609
↑	↑	↑	↑
Volume	State Court	Series	Page Number

In this example, you would first locate the set of books marked "Illinois Appellate, Third Series." Then you would locate volume 216, and turn to page 609. On page 609 of volume 216 of Illinois Appellate 3d case reporter you would find the appellate court opinion in *People v. Wheeler*, decided in 1992. (This same case would also be found on page 1326 of volume 575 of the Northeastern Reporter, Second Series.)

If *People v. Wheeler* has been appealed to a higher state or federal court, there are other sets of books (called *Shepard's Citations*) that will lead you to the later case reporter citations.

For more information about legal research, see the book *Legal Research Made Easy*, by Suzan Herskowitz published by Sphinx Publishing, available through Sourcebooks, Inc.

The following resources are national agencies and organizations which may be able to help obtain assistance.

Child Find of America, Inc.
    P.O. Box 277
    New Paltz, N.Y. 12561
    (914)255-1848
    (800)I-AM-LOST
    (800)A-WAY-OUT

    Child Find's objective is to find missing children. There is no fee for investigations of missing children.

Kemp National Center for the Prevention and Treatment of Child Abuse and Neglect
    1205 Oneida
    Denver, C.O. 80220
    (305)321-3963

    The Center provides information on child abuse and prevention.

Kidsrights
    10100 Park Cedar Drive
    Charlotte, N.C. 28210
    (800)892-KIDS

    Kidsrights' objective is to provide information regarding child molestation, child abuse, teen rape and suicide, drug abuse, self-esteem, AIDS and related children's rights issues.

Mothers Against Drunk Driving (MADD)
    511 East John Carpenter Freeway
    Suite 700
    Irving, T.X. 75062

    MADD's national office can provide information regarding drunk driving, and referral to chapters in all 50 states.

National Commission Against Drunk Driving
> 1910 K Street N.W.
> Suite 810
> Washington D.C. 20006
> (202)452-6004

> The Commission offers general informational referrals on motor vehicle-related statistics, programs, and legislation.

National Committee for Prevention of Child Abuse
> 322 South Michigan Ave.
> Suite 1600
> Chicago, I.L. 60604
> (312)663-3520

> The Committee educates the public about child abuse and offers information and referral to chapters in all 50 states.

National Victim Center
> 2111 Wilson Blvd.
> Suite 300
> Arlington, V.A. 22201
> (800)FYI-CALL
> (703)276-2880

> The Center has facilities in Virginia and Texas. It promotes victims' rights and victim assistance. It can provide information on legislation information.

National Organization for Victim Assistance (NOVA)
> 1757 Park Road N.W.
> Washington, D.C. 20010
> (800)879-NOVA
> (202)232-6682

> NOVA advocates for victim-oriented legislation at the national, state and local levels. Its library is open to the public by appointment.

U.S. Dept of Health and Human Services—National Center on Child Abuse and Neglect
P.O. Box 1182
Washington, D.C. 20013
(703)385-7565

A reading room is available to the public.

Additional Toll-free Hotline Information

National Center for Missing and Exploited Children (800)843-5678

National Clearinghouse on Child Abuse and Neglect (800)394-3366

National Domestic Violence Hotline (800)799-7233
  • ttd/tty (800)787-3224 for the hearing impaired

National Resource Center on Child Abuse and Neglect (800)227-5242

National Resource Center on Child Sexual Abuse (800)543-7006

National Resource Center on Domestic Violence (800)537-2238

ENDNOTES

1. See Bureau of Justice Statistics. Violent Crime: Selected Findings. (U.S. Dept. of Justice, Wash. D.C. Govt Prntg Office, April, 1994).
2. *Cox Broadcasting Corp. v. Cohn*, 420 U.S. 469 (1975).
3. See Appendix B, Pennsylvania listing.
4. See Appendix B, Ohio listing.
5. Ziegenmeyer, N. "Taking Back My Life." Ladies Home Journal (Feb. 92), p. 130.
6. "Inside People" People Weekly. (4.3.95), p. 6 (1994 Milton Petrie Award).
7. The Des Moines Register won for publishing Nancy Zegenmeyer's story. See Newsweek "Naming Names," p. 27.
8. These rights were set out in the case of *Miranda v. Arizona*, 384 U.S. 436 (1966).
9. "Sex Offender Registration Laws," National Victim Center (1995).
10. For more indepth coverage of crime victim compensation see Ginsburg, W., *Victims' Rights: The Complete Guide to Crime Victim Compensation* (1994).
11. "Restitution" usually means returning something of value to the victim whereas "reparation" may include other damages which are easily measurable.
12. *Wassell v. Adams*, 865 F.2d 849 (7th Cir. 1989).
13. See Appendix B for a representative listing of state limitation statutes.
14. *Jamieson v. Hickey*, 199 Cal. App. 3d 595, 244 Cal. Rptr. 859 (1988).
15. See generally "Son of Sam" laws regulating or prohibiting distribution of crime-related book, film, or comparable revenues to criminals, validity, construction, and application of, 60 A.L.R. 4th 1210.
16. See *Simon & Schuster v. Crime Victims Bd.*, 502 U.S. 105, 116 LEd. 2d 476, 112 S. Ct. 501 (1991).
17. See the U.S. Bankruptcy Code, 11 U.S.C. Sec. 523(a).
18. See 11 U.S.C. 1301 (Chapter 13).
19. *Urie v. Thompson*, 337 U.S. 163, 93 L.Ed. 1282 (1949) (plaintiff inhaled silia dust which manifested the disease of silicosis some fifteen years later).
20. See generally, Note, Civil Claims of Adults Molested as Children; Maturation of Harm and the Statute of Limitations Hurdle 1986-87, Fordham Urban L.J. 709 (1987).
21. Id., at 727.
22. *Tyson v. Tyson*, 107 Wash. 2d 72, 727 P.2d 226 (1986).
23. The *Tyson* case has been superseded by statute RCW 4.16.350.
24. *EW v. DCH*, 231 Mont. 481, 754 P.2d 817 (1988).
25. See e.g., *DeRose v. Carswell*, 196 Cal. App. 3d 1011, 242 Cal. Rptr. 368 (1987); and *Evans v. Eckelman*, 216 Cal. App. 3d 1609, 265 Cal. Rptr. 605 (1990).
26. *Hammer v. Hammer*, 142 Wis. 2d 257, 418 N.W. 2d 23 (1987) reh. den. 133 Wis. 2d 953, 428 N.W. 2d 552 (1998).
27. See Appendix B.

28. See Glazer, S., "Violence Against Women," CQ Researcher Congressional Quarterly Inc., p. 171, vol. 3, no. 8 (February, 1993).

29. Bureau of Justice Statistics (BJS), "Wives are the most frequent victims in family murders" press release, Bureau of Justice Statistics, United States Department of Justice, July 10, 1994.

30. American Bar Association, "The Impact of Domestic Violence on Children: A Report to the President of the ABA (Oct 1994)

31. *DeShaney v. Winnebago County Dept. of Social Services*, 489 U.S. 187 (1989). (State had no responsibility to protect child while in custody of his father.)

32. See *Jordan v. City of Rome*, 417 S.E. 2d 730 (Ga. App., 1992). But some cases have been successful against police where the dispatcher was negligent, *DeLong v. Erie County*, 457 N.E. 2d 717 (New York, 1983).

33. See *Baker v. City of New York*, 25 A.D. 2d 770, 269 N.Y.S. 2d 515 (1966); *Jensen v. South Carolina Dept. of Social Services*, 297 S.C. 323, 377 S.E.2d 102 (1988); *Coffman v. Wilson Police Department*, 739 F. Supp. 257 (E.D. Pa., 1990).

34. *Calloway v. Kinkelaar*, 168 Ill.2d 312, 659 N.E.2d 1322 (1995).

35. Id., at 677-678, 659 N.E.2d 1324-25.

36. *Sorichetti v. City of New York*, 65 N.Y.2d 461, 482 N.E. 2d 70 (1985).

Index

A

Accountability, 8
Alternate Dispute Resolution (ADR), 130
Answer, 124
Appeal, 89–90, 135
Arraignment, 56
Arrest, 47
Attorneys, (see "Lawyers")

B

Bail, 21, 56–59, 89
Bench trial, 54, 67, 77
"Beyond a reasonable doubt," 9, 96
Bill of rights, 23
Bond, 56–58, 89
Burden of proof, 102

C

Case management, 27–29
Causation, 104–105
Charges, 49–50
Civil complaint, 164
Civil suit, 99
    elements, 102
    theories, 102–104
Closing statement, 73, 133
Commercial carriers, 145
Compensation, 26, 98
Complaint, 118
Constitutional rights, 23
Counseling, 14–17
Crime scene, 41
Cross examination, 69–70

D

Damages, 107, 134
    compensatory, 107
    punitive, 107
Day care, 149
Defenses, 10, 105
    entrapment, 11
    factual, 106
    identification, 11
    insanity, 12
    jurisdiction, 106
    parties, 106
    self-defense, 11
    sexual assault cases, 11
Depositions, 126
Direct examination, 69
Discovery, 125
    deposition, 126
    interrogatory, 126
Domestic violence, 9, 21, 143
Double jeopardy, 76, 89
Duty, 121
    reasonable care, 103

E

Elements of crime, 7
Employer, 146
Escape of the offender, 92
Evidence, 68
    DNA, 46

F

Family members,
     offender, 9, 101
     effect on, 19
Felony, 6–7, 49–50
Fifth Amendment, 9
Filing a civil suit, 114–115
First Amendment, 31–32
Foreseeability, 105

G

Government, 150
Grand jury, 51

H

Harassment, 25
Hospitals, 149
Hotel or motel, 147

I

Identification of offender,
     lineup, 45–46
     show up, 45
     unknown, 46
Insurance, 98
Interrogatories, 126
Interview, victim, 39–40
Intimidation, 25
Intra-spousal immunity, 101
Investigation, 39
     detectives, 42

J

Judge, 53
Judgment, 134
     enforcing, 135
Jurisdiction, 106, 115, 119
Jury, 75–76
     hung, 76
     trial, 67–68
Juveniles, 8, 100

L

Landlords, 147–148
Lawyers, 151
     confidentiality, 152
     fee agreements, 154
Legal research, 199

M

Media, 33
Miranda rights, 47
Misdemeanor, 6, 49
Motions,
     change of judge, 61
     change of venue, 61
     continuance, 61
     discovery, 60–61, 125
     dismiss, 60
     suppress, 61

O

Opening Statement, 68, 131

P

Petty offenses, 6
Planes, 145
Plea, 56
     guilty but mentally ill, 12, 76
     no contest, 56
     nolo contendere, 56
Plea bargains, 63
Police, 150
Preliminary hearing, 22, 51, 60
Preponderance of the evidence, 95, 102
Presidential Task Force, 20
Pre-trial motions (also see "motions"), 60
Privacy, 31, 119
Procedures, 64
Property, return of, 26

R

Release of the offender, 92
Reparation, 98
Reporting the crime, 35
     contacting the police, 36
     hospital and medical personnel, 36
Request letter for prisoner information, 159
Request letter to police, 157
Request letter to prosecutor, 158
Resources, 201
Restaurants, 148
Restitution, 26, 82, 98

S

Schools, 149
Sentencing,
    commutation, 92
    determinate, 79
    dispositions,79
    execution, 80
    fines, 83
    imprisonment, 80
    indeterminate, 79
    pardon, 92
    parole, 92
    presentence investigation, 83
    probation, 81
    restitution, 26, 82
    supervision, 82
    violation, 88
Settlement, 128–130
Sexual abuse, 139
Sexual assault, 11, 137
Shopping centers, 148
Sixth Amendment, 10
Speedy trial, 55
Standard of proof, 95–96
State laws, 167–197
Statute of limitations, 51–52, 114
Subpoena, 128
Summons, 122

T

Testimony, 68, 72, 96
Third party defendant, 101, 104, 143, 145
Time limits, 51–52
Tort, 27, 103
    intentional, 102
Trains, 145

V

Verdict, 77, 134
Victim Impact Statement, 25, 65, 84–87, 93, 160
Victims of Crime Act (VOCA), 14
Voir dire, 67

W

Witnesses, 20, 71
Wrongful death, 100

Your #1 Source for Real World Legal Information...

LEGAL SURVIVAL GUIDES™

• Written by lawyers
• Simple English explanation of the law
• Forms and instructions included

HELP YOUR LAWYER WIN YOUR CASE

Even with a lawyer, what you know may determine whether you win or lose, and how much it will cost you. This book shows you how to save money, and help win your case. Topics include: selecting a lawyer, giving your lawyer good information, asking the right questions, understanding the system, and helping your lawyer prepare your case.

156 pages; $12.95;
ISBN 1-57248-021-1

VICTIMS' RIGHTS

The financial loss from crime can devastate the victim and his or her family. Medical and psychological treatment costs can far exceed any property loss. Now, crime victims anywhere in the U.S. can find out how to obtain compensation for these losses.

163 pages; $12.95;
ISBN 0-913825-82-4

NEIGHBOR VS. NEIGHBOR

This entertaining book explains constitutional rights, zoning laws, private restrictions, and how these affect neighbor disputes.

229 pages; $12.95;
ISBN 0-913825-41-7

What our customers say about our books:

"It couldn't be more clear for the lay person." —R.D.

"I want you to know I really appreciate your book. It has saved me a lot of time and money." —L.T.

"Your real estate contracts book has saved me nearly $12,000.00 in closing costs over the past year." —A.B.

"...many of the legal questions that I have had over the years were answered clearly and concisely through your plain English interpretation of the law." —C.E.H.

"If there weren't people out there like you I'd be lost. You have the best books of this type out there." —S.B.

"...your forms and directions are easy to follow." —C.V.M.

Legal Survival Guides are directly available from the publisher, or from your local bookstores.
For credit card orders call 1–800–43–BRIGHT, write P.O. Box 372, Naperville, IL 60566,
or fax 630-961-2168

LEGAL SURVIVAL GUIDES™ NATIONAL TITLES
Valid in All 50 States

LEGAL SURVIVAL IN BUSINESS

How to Form Your Own Corporation (2E)	$19.95
How to Register Your Own Copyright (2E)	$19.95
How to Register Your Own Trademark (2E)	$19.95
Most Valuable Business Forms You'll Ever Need	$19.95
Most Valuable Corporate Forms You'll Ever Need	$24.95
Software Law (with diskette)	$29.95

LEGAL SURVIVAL IN COURT

Crime Victim's Guide to Justice	$19.95
Debtors' Rights (2E)	$12.95
Defend Yourself Against Criminal Charges	$19.95
Grandparents' Rights	$19.95
Help Your Lawyer Win Your Case	$12.95
Jurors' Rights	$9.95
Legal Malpractice and Other Claims Against Your Lawyer	$18.95
Legal Research Made Easy	$14.95
Simple Ways to Protect Yourself From Lawsuits	$24.95
Victim's Rights	$12.95
Winning Your Personal Injury Claim	$19.95

LEGAL SURVIVAL IN REAL ESTATE

How to Buy a Condominium or Townhome	$16.95
How to Negotiate Real Estate Contracts (2E)	$16.95
How to Negotiate Real Estate Leases (2E)	$16.95
Successful Real Estate Brokerage Management	$19.95

LEGAL SURVIVAL IN PERSONAL AFFAIRS

How to File Your Own Bankruptcy (4E)	$19.95
How to File Your Own Divorce (3E)	$19.95
How to Make Your Own Will	$12.95
How to Write Your Own Living Will	$9.95
Living Trusts and Simple Ways to Avoid Probate	$19.95
Neighbor vs. Neighbor	$12.95
Power of Attorney Handbook (2E)	$19.95
Social Security Benefits Handbook	$14.95
U.S.A. Immigration Guide (2E)	$19.95
Guia de Inmigracion a Estados Unidos	$19.95

Legal Survival Guides are directly available from the publisher, or from your local bookstores.

For credit card orders call 1–800–43–BRIGHT, write P.O. Box 372, Naperville, IL 60566, or fax 630-961-2168

LEGAL SURVIVAL GUIDES™ STATE TITLES

Up-to-date for Your State

NEW YORK

How to File for Divorce in NY	$19.95
How to Make a NY Will	$12.95
How to Start a Business in NY	$16.95
How to Win in Small Claims Court in NY	$14.95
Landlord's Rights and Duties in NY	$19.95
New York Power of Attorney Handbook	$12.95

PENNSYLVANIA

How to File for Divorce in PA	$19.95
How to Make a PA Will	$12.95
How to Start a Business in PA	$16.95
Landlord's Rights and Duties in PA	$19.95

FLORIDA

Florida Power of Attorney Handbook	$9.95
How to Change Your Name in FL (3E)	$14.95
How to File a FL Construction Lien (2E)	$19.95
How to File a Guardianship in FL	$19.95
How to File for Divorce in FL (4E)	$21.95
How to Form a Nonprofit Corp in FL (3E)	$19.95
How to Form a Simple Corp in FL (3E)	$19.95
How to Make a FL Will (4E)	$9.95
How to Modify Your FL Divorce Judgement (3E)	$22.95
How to Probate an Estate in FL (2E)	$24.95
How to Start a Business in FL (4E)	$16.95
How to Win in Small Claims Court in FL (5E)	$14.95
Land Trusts in FL (4E)	$24.95
Landlord's Rights and Duties in FL (6E)	$19.95
Women's Legal Rights in FL	$19.95

GEORGIA

How to File for Divorce in GA (2E)	$19.95
How to Make a GA Will (2E)	$9.95
How to Start and Run a GA Business (2E)	$18.95

ILLINOIS

How to File for Divorce in IL	$19.95
How to Make an IL Will	$9.95
How to Start a Business in IL	$16.95

MASSACHUSETTS

How to File for Divorce in MA	$19.95
How to Make a MA Will	$9.95
How to Probate an Estate in MA	$19.95
How to Start a Business in MA	$16.95
Landlord's Rights and Duties in MA	$19.95

MICHIGAN

How to File for Divorce in MI	$19.95
How to Make a MI Will	$9.95
How to Start a Business in MI	$16.95

MINNESOTA

How to File for Divorce in MN	$19.95
How to Form a Simple Corporation in MN	$19.95
How to Make a MN Will	$9.95
How to Start a Business in MN	$16.95

NORTH CAROLINA

How to File for Divorce in NC	$19.95
How to Make a NC Will	$9.95
How to Start a Business in NC	$16.95

TEXAS

How to File for Divorce in TX	$19.95
How to Form a Simple Corporation in TX	$19.95
How to Make a TX Will	$9.95
How to Probate an Estate in TX	$19.95
How to Start a Business in TX	$16.95
How to Win in Small Claims Court in TX	$14.95
Landlord's Rights and Duties in TX	$19.95

Legal Survival Guides are directly available from the publisher, or from your local bookstores.

For credit card orders call 1–800–43–BRIGHT, write P.O. Box 372, Naperville, IL 60566,
or fax 630-961-2168

Legal Survival Guides™ • Order Form

Qty	ISBN	Title	Retail
		Legal Survival Guides Fall 97 National Frontlist	
	1-57071-223-9	How to File Your Own Bankruptcy (4E)	$19.95
	1-57071-224-7	How to File Your Own Divorce (3E)	$19.95
	1-57071-227-1	How to Form Your Own Corporation (2E)	$19.95
	1-57071-228-X	How to Make Your Own Will	$12.95
	1-57071-225-5	How to Register Your Own Copyright (2E)	$19.95
	1-57071-226-3	How to Register Your Own Trademark (2E)	$19.95
		Fall 97 New York Frontlist	
	1-57071-184-4	How to File for Divorce in NY	$19.95
	1-57071-183-6	How to Make a NY Will	$12.95
	1-57071-185-2	How to Start a Business in NY	$16.95
	1-57071-187-9	How to Win in Small Claims Court in NY	$14.95
	1-57071-186-0	Landlord's Rights and Duties in NY	$19.95
	1-57071-188-7	New York Power of Attorney Handbook	$12.95
		Fall 97 Pennsylvania Frontlist	
	1-57071-177-1	How to File for Divorce in PA	$19.95
	1-57071-176-3	How to Make a PA Will	$12.95
	1-57071-178-X	How to Start a Business in PA	$16.95
	1-57071-179-8	Landlord's Rights and Duties in PA	$19.95
		Legal Survival Guides National Backlist	
	1-57071-166-6	Crime Victim's Guide to Justice	$19.95
	1-57248-023-8	Debtors' Rights (2E)	$12.95
	1-57071-162-3	Defend Yourself Against Criminal Charges	$19.95
	1-57248-001-7	Grandparents' Rights	$19.95
	0-913825-99-9	Guia de Inmigracion a Estados Unidos	$19.95
	1-57248-021-1	Help Your Lawyer Win Your Case	$12.95
	1-57071-164-X	How to Buy a Condominium or Townhome	$16.95
	1-57248-035-1	How to Negotiate Real Estate Contracts (2E)	$16.95
	1-57248-036-X	How to Negotiate Real Estate Leases (2E)	$16.95
	1-57071-167-4	How to Write Your Own Living Will	$9.95
	1-57248-031-9	Jurors' Rights	$9.95
	1-57248-032-7	Legal Malpractice and Other Claims Against Your Lawyer	$18.95
	1-57248-008-4	Legal Research Made Easy	$14.95
	1-57248-019-X	Living Trusts and Simple Ways to Avoid Probate	$19.95
	1-57248-022-X	Most Valuable Business Forms You'll Ever Need	$19.95
	1-57248-007-6	Most Valuable Corporate Forms You'll Ever Need	$24.95
	0-913825-41-7	Neighbor vs. Neighbor	$12.95
	1-57248-044-0	Power of Attorney Handbook (2E)	$19.95
	1-57248-020-3	Simple Ways to Protect Yourself From Lawsuits	$24.95
	1-57248-033-5	Social Security Benefits Handbook	$14.95
	1-57071-163-1	Software Law (w/diskette)	$29.95
	0-913825-86-7	Successful Real Estate Brokerage Mgmt.	$19.95
	1-57248-000-9	U.S.A. Immigration Guide (2E)	$19.95
	0-913825-82-4	Victim's Rights	$12.95
	1-57071-165-8	Winning Your Personal Injury Claim	$19.95
		Florida Backlist	
	0-913825-81-6	Florida Power of Attorney Handbook	$9.95
	1-57248-028-9	How to Change Your Name in FL (3E)	$14.95
	0-913825-84-0	How to File a FL Construction Lien (2E)	$19.95
	0-913825-53-0	How to File a Guardianship in FL	$19.95
	1-57248-046-7	How to File for Divorce in FL (4E)	$21.95

Qty	ISBN	Title	Retail
		Florida Backlist (cont')	
	1-57248-004-1	How to Form a Nonprofit Corp in FL (3E)	$19.95
	0-913825-96-4	How to Form a Simple Corp in FL (3E)	$19.95
	1-57248-027-0	How to Make a FL Will (4E)	$9.95
	1-57248-056-4	How to Modify Your FL Divorce Judgement (3E)	$22.95
	1-57248-003-3	How to Probate an Estate in FL (2E)	$24.95
	1-57248-005-X	How to Start a Business in FL (4E)	$16.95
	0-913825-97-2	How to Win in Small Claims Court in FL (5E)	$14.95
	1-57248-029-7	Land Trusts in FL (4E)	$24.95
	1-57248-057-2	Landlord's Rights and Duties in FL (6E)	$19.95
	0-913825-73-5	Women's Legal Rights in FL	$19.95
		Georgia Backlist	
	1-57248-058-0	How to File for Divorce in GA (2E)	$19.95
	1-57248-047-5	How to Make a GA Will (2E)	$9.95
	1-57248-026-2	How to Start and Run a GA Business (2E)	$18.95
		Illinois Backlist	
	1-57248-042-4	How to File for Divorce in IL	$19.95
	1-57248-043-2	How to Make an IL Will	$9.95
	1-57248-041-6	How to Start a Business in IL	$16.95
		Massachusetts Backlist	
	1-57248-051-3	How to File for Divorce in MA	$19.95
	1-57248-050-5	How to Make a MA Will	$9.95
	1-57248-053-X	How to Probate an Estate in MA	$19.95
	1-57248-054-8	How to Start a Business in MA	$16.95
	1-57248-055-6	Landlord's Rights and Duties in MA	$19.95
		Michigan Backlist	
	1-57248-014-9	How to File for Divorce in MI	$19.95
	1-57248-015-7	How to Make a MI Will	$9.95
	1-57248-013-0	How to Start a Business in MI	$16.95
		Minnesota Backlist	
	1-57248-039-4	How to File for Divorce in MN	$19.95
	1-57248-040-8	How to Form a Simple Corporation in MN	$19.95
	1-57248-037-8	How to Make a MN Will	$9.95
	1-57248-038-6	How to Start a Business in MN	$16.95
		North Carolina Backlist	
	0-913825-94-8	How to File for Divorce in NC	$19.95
	0-913825-92-1	How to Make a NC Will	$9.95
	0-913825-93-X	How to Start a Business in NC	$16.95
		Texas Backlist	
	0-913825-91-3	How to File for Divorce in TX	$19.95
	1-57248-009-2	How to Form a Simple Corporation in TX	$19.95
	0-913825-89-1	How to Make a TX Will	$9.95
	1-57248-010-6	How to Probate an Estate in TX	$19.95
	0-913825-90-5	How to Start a Business in TX	$16.95
	1-57248-012-2	How to Win in Small Claims Court in TX	$14.95
	1-57248-011-4	Landlord's Rights and Duties in TX	$19.95
		SUBTOTAL	
		IL Residents add 6.75%, FL Residents add county sales tax	
		Shipping— $4.00 for 1st book, $1.00 each additional	
		Total	

To order, call Sourcebooks at 1-800-43-BRIGHT or FAX (630)961-2168 (Bookstores, libraries, wholesalers—please call for discount)